Evangelism Intelligence: Why Adventist Churches Grow Differently

ROGER WALTER, DMIN.

FLAMING ARROW PUBLISHERS

Copyright © 2018 Roger Walter

ISBN: 978-0-692-10522-1

DEDICATION

This book is dedicated to my wife, Gail, and my kids:
Seth, Krista, Grayson, Kylie, Summer, Kinsee, Sydney, Kozette
and Christian. This incredible family of mine represents those who
currently reach people with the message of Jesus and the next
generation who are being shot out like flaming arrows, to ignite
the world for Christ!

CONTENTS

ACKNOWLEDGEMENTS

I want to thank Gail, my wife, for whom this book would have never gotten off the ground or completed. She's a hard driver, and I love her tremendously. Thank you to those who gave me ideas, read early manuscripts and gave me feedback – Dave Livermore, Hiram Rester, Jared Spano, Bradley Nunn and Nick Jones. A special thank you to the editing skills of Mary Jo Cannard and Vivian Pena for their help thinking through my fuzzy writing skills. Their feedback was invaluable to this process. Thank you also to my wife Gail and my daughter Summer who worked on the graphic design of this with me. I also want to thank the many pastors I have coached over the years who have let me try out these ideas on them and see them work. Finally, I want to thank the church members in Lebanon and Sweet Home, Oregon; at The Adventure in Greeley, Colorado; and now the Adventist Community Church in Vancouver, Washington for allowing us to make a difference in reaching people for the kingdom. It has a been an amazing pleasure to be your pastor.

Introduction: Evangelism Intelligence

"Our evangelistic efforts only teach doctrine, and never Christ and Him crucified. Our evangelism doesn't work in making Christians," my instructor proclaimed.

I was stunned. I sat there speechless as he pontificated a bit more. Where did he get this great pronouncement? Why did he feel the need to assault evangelism in a class on personal spirituality?

This was a professor I respected a lot. I had taken classes from him in my undergraduate work and was now again as I worked on my doctorate. What he said, was off topic for the class, it was a bit of an aside. His expertise was in Old Testament and personal spirituality. Yet, the respect he held gave it much more credibility in many student's minds than it normally would. Based on my experience, it was also flat-out wrong. In fact, it was way out in left-field.

I can never keep my mouth shut, and I could not let it go, even if it appeared disrespectful of a teacher. I tentatively raised my hand and as calmly as I could, trying not to be impolite, said, "I see things differently. My experience has been that evangelism does work. I have done a lot of evangelism and I have seen a lot of success with it. My experience is that the very core of evangelism is about Jesus and Him crucified. When that is left out, then it doesn't work."

This book is really about that central core of Jesus. I call it Evangelism Intelligence. Its aim is to help people see that evangelism does work; that it continues to preach Jesus Christ and Him crucified.

For the sake of this book, we are using the term evangelism for a reaping meeting, prophecy seminar, or any other decision-getting meeting that the church engages in to reach the community. Obviously, there are many things that go into making these a success, and we are going to cover those things as we go.

They Leave, We Stay

My good friend Bill called me a few years ago. His church and the surrounding churches were having an area-wide evangelistic series with a famous Adventist speaker. The series was being held at Bill's church. It was a very large church. Bill had never done much evangelism in his ministry. He had pastored mostly large churches that did not want to do traditional evangelism, so he did not feel like he knew what to expect. As the seminar progressed, he was not sure he liked it all that much. As we talked, he said, "The seminar is going okay, but I don't like some of what is going on. In fact, I strongly disagree with some of what is being done."

"Me too!" I quipped. "I rarely agree with my evangelists on everything they do, or how they choose to do it."

"What?" He choked. "But you do a lot of evangelism! How is that?"

"It's true that we do a lot of evangelism, yet there are many things that happen in an evangelistic series that I do not agree with. In the end, the evangelist leaves and I get to keep the church and continue to shape it. I get to lead these new people in the way God directs. We work through all those other things over time. In the end, Jesus still shines."

I went on to explain to my friend that an evangelistic seminar is not going to teach everything. That, like all of us, evangelists usually have quirky and dysfunctional characteristics. However, the key point to focus on and remember is: evangelism is about getting people to make decisions for Jesus. It's not about the evangelist – he is not the message. The reason I put up with some of the quirkiness is because an experienced evangelist knows how to get more decisions. When the evangelist leaves, I get to stay and we can get over some of the oddities. I get to shape the church and the new people. I get the best of both worlds: new people through decisions and the ability to shape those new people into grace-filled Adventist Christians.

I believe that when Jesus comes again, the only spiritual gift we quit using is the gift of evangelism. That is what Evangelism Intelligence is about. Evangelism Intelligence helps us see clearly the purpose of evangelism and making it work in our context.

Evangelism Intelligence

In his books on Emotional Intelligence, Daniel Goleman writes on the idea of understanding our emotions and how others respond emotionally. This has raised up a whole industry of people writing books that talk about, deal with, and seek to explain how emotions function in the workplace and in life. I learned a lot about myself and about how to work with other people from Goleman.

This book is clearly a throwback to Goleman's work, yet, I do not seek for us to understand our emotional side, but rather our very important work in evangelism. Evangelism Intelligence means that there are clear, logical things to do and not to do, that make evangelism work. Evangelism intelligence is about giving insight to you, the reader, who might not otherwise know the best way to do things. Evangelism Intelligence is about breaking down the growing barrier that actually stops us from doing evangelism.

Pastors have traditionally been called upon to either organize or conduct evangelism in their church. Yet, fewer and fewer pastors seem to think it works. Fewer and fewer seminary professors think it works. I have had at least five seminary professors in my doctoral and masters work tell the class that evangelism does not work the way we have always done it and that it was only teaching doctrine, only teaching facts and not talking about Jesus. I have had as many conference presidents tell me the same thing. I have done my very best to prove them wrong and I believe that saying "evangelism doesn't work" is an urban myth. We will get to that in Chapter 4.

This book, and my comments following my teacher's pronouncement, is about disproving that myth that evangelism does not work. I believe that anyone can do evangelism, successfully, and not have to have bad feelings about the evangelist or think that we are only turning the "metho-pisto-bapti-terians[1]" into Adventists.

Evangelism Intelligence is about knowing what you are getting yourself into and knowing how to successfully operate an evangelistic meeting. It is about debunking the myths that continue to perpetuate themselves. Evangelism Intelligence is knowing the issues that work and those that do not. How do I know that this is the case? Because I have seen evangelism work in every church I have pastored – as an associate pastor, as a pastor of a two-church district, then in a contemporary church plant and now a large multi-staff church in a metro area.

What I am going to show in this book helped take two of my churches to score in the top ten for fastest growing churches in the North American Division (NAD). Another one would have made that list also, except it was two churches and counted separately. It works in all the churches I have pastored, coached or consulted over a period of more than 25 years. I have pastored in the contemporary church plant, in a traditional large, multi-staff church, and in a two-church district.

According to the Adventist Statistical Website[2], the average church in the NAD baptizes six people per year. I work in Oregon, and our baptismal averages are identical to the national average. When I asked my former Conference President about it, he said, "If you take the ethnic churches out of the mix, that number decreases to three per year."[3]

My father-in-law is a pastor in another conference that pushes its pastors to do yearly evangelism. They often have the whole conference doing an evangelistic series at the same time. I applaud this. Yet, according to the same statistical website, their conference has essentially the same number of baptisms as the national average.[4]

---

[1] A catch-phrase I heard a long time ago to smash the words Methodists, Episcopal, Baptist, and Presbyterians together. A term simply expressing the "already convinced."
[2] see www.adventiststatistics.org
[3] from a conversation with my then conference president, Al Reimche.
[4] We will get into why I believe their evangelism is not working as well as it could, in a later chapter.

To put this all in perspective, imagine my conference has 120 churches. Statistically that would be approximately 720 baptisms a year. If we take out the ethnic churches that make up for half of those baptisms. We are left with 360 baptisms for the remaining churches to divide. Then take out a church like mine, where we baptize between 30-40 per year. It becomes clear that some churches are not baptizing anyone! In other words, there are some churches that never see an adult baptism. Then, you add the aging population of our churches that is approaching 55+ and that means that many of our churches have no kids. Therefore, they never have to check the plumbing on the baptistery to see if it still works.

I attended a pastors' meeting early in my ministry. That year, my two churches had close to 100 baptisms. During the course of the week, the President of the conference applauded one pastor who had taken his church from 700 members to over 1,000 members that year. Wow! On the surface it seems like a huge accomplishment. Now, I loved this pastoral colleague of mine. He is a great pastor and pastored a great church. Internally though, I laughed and cried. Sure, the growth of that church was incredible. Adding 300 new members is pretty amazing. We do not see that often. However, when you understand the dynamics that led to that growth, it was not nearly as amazing as the numbers might appear.

Here is the back story: another church in the same metro area was the largest church in the conference. That church went through some horrible internal conflicts and more than two-thirds of the active members fled to other area churches. The largest number of people, 300, landed on the doorstep of my friend's church who was applauded above. His growth was literally from the transfer of members from the flailing church across town. I know this to be true, because I was close friends with the associate pastors on staff at both of these churches.

Literally, the church that my conference president applauded, had a total of 6 baptisms that year! They were now the largest church in the conference. They had some incredible growth, but their baptismal rate was the national average. It just seemed to me that if the average church is about 75-100 people and they average 6 baptisms a year, a church of 1,000 should get even more, right?

My goal in sharing this is not to say negative things about a pastoral friend and colleague or about his church. Rather, my aim is to show a dynamic that seems to be prevalent in our churches. That dynamic simply says, "As long as our membership numbers keep rising, we're doing a great work." I am not always sure I agree.

Mike Regele, in his book "Death of the Church," says that most churches simply switch members from one denomination to another.[5] I sat there and said to myself, "I want to grow my church, but I want it to be about Kingdom growth, not transfer growth. I want to see every church grow, but not by trading members around." There are legitimate reasons to take members in on transfer of membership. However, Kingdom growth is about evangelistic growth not transfer growth.

In this book, you will see my assertion: *The Great Commission is what the church should be about*. My hope is that with this book, you will be able to gain some fresh insight into WHY evangelism works and HOW to make it happen in your church. It is my prayer, that this book will give us some insight into Evangelism Intelligence. It's why Adventist churches grow differently.

---

[5] Regele, Mike, (1995) *Death of the Church* (p. 154-160) Zondervan Publishing

1

How It All Begins

BANG! BANG! BANG! BANG!

The loud knocking on my front door sent my 12-year-old legs running to see what was going on. When I got to the door, two men in ties were standing there asking if Sharon was there. That was my mom, so I went running to get her.

"Mom! Two men want to talk with you at the door!" I excitedly said.

"What do they want? I don't have time for a salesman," she whined. But she went to the door wiping her hands on a towel as she passed through the kitchen.

"Hi! Sharon? We are just out inviting people to come to an upcoming seminar on the Bible starting in just a few weeks. We wanted to make sure you had a personal invite to come. Here is the brochure."

The two men, as it turns out, were college-aged, ministerial students working with the Oregon Conference evangelist that summer. They were out inviting former Adventists and non-attending Adventists to come to their evangelistic meetings. That is why they invited my mom. In all the years she had been gone from church – nearly 20 years – the Stone Tower Church had never removed my mom's name from membership.

Both of my parents were raised in the Seventh-day Adventist Church. My dad was raised in a strict, almost legalistic environment. My mom was raised in a liberal, almost passive environment. Both had left the church right out of high school. They met after they had both stopped going to church.

My brother who was 16, at the time, and I knew almost nothing about church, God, religion, or anything else. The only times I really went to church in my first 12 years was for a couple of weddings.

One time when we went to church and someone opened up part of the wall and it looked like a puppet show was about to appear. Both participants were wearing blue robes. Then one of them pushed the other one down below sight and all of a sudden, he came back up wet! I was about 4 years old, had never seen a baptism before and had no idea what that was about. The only other time I remember going to church, they served a snack, but I was not allowed to have that little glass of juice and the cracker they were serving. I decided right then and there, church was not for me. They were too selfish to even share their snacks.

When I was growing up, the only time I heard the name of Jesus was as a swear word. I had no concept of what grace was – that was the really long prayer-thing my grandpa did at Thanksgiving, right? I had never heard of the Lamb of God which takes away the sin of the world. All that was about to change.

After the two college students left, my mom stood there looking at the brochure in her hand. She knew exactly what it was, she grew up with this type of thing. My mom's thought process floated in her head. Something like this:

"Gary is going to be a Junior in High School this year, and he probably ought to have a little religion before he leaves home. Right now, he basically has none. After high school, then what? How can I get Von (my dad) to agree to go though?"

That evening, my dad came home to a well-cooked meal and a family all ready for him because my mom had talked to us, and she made the seminar sound interesting. My dad had seen the brochure on the counter before anyone said anything. He knew exactly what it was, but he did not pick it up. In fact, he ignored it.

During the meal, my mom started talking about the seminar, what sounded interesting about it, where it was and the time. Then she dropped her request, "Don't you think we should at least introduce the boys to some of the religion we were raised with?"

Surprisingly, my dad agreed. He thought it could not hurt to go to two or three of the meetings, then quit. My mom was in shock when he agreed to go.

My dad used to invite the Jehovah's Witnesses in when they came to the house. He would argue with them about what the Bible said, as he sat there with a cigarette in one hand and a beer in the other. He knew his Bible from his childhood. Once when my mom wanted to take us to a VBS at the local Lutheran Church, my dad said, "Absolutely not! If my boys go to any church, it'll be an Adventist Church!" Of course, he refused to go each time my mom suggested attending.

That first week after my dad agreed to attend the seminar, my mom decided to attend church. The seminar was still a week or so away. She dragged me off to church with her.

"Mom! Why do I have to go to church? Why can't I stay home and watch the game with dad? That's what we always do! It's great father-son time, Mom! Moooo-ooooommmmm! Don't you know the best cartoons come on Saturday and they start in just a few minutes?"

I sat through my first real church service at 12 years of age. I remember nothing about it. I know they met in a Friend's Church, and I can still visualize that church in my head. As we were leaving, and our row was dismissed, I was looking around trying to take it all in.

THUMP!

Someone had just thumped my chest! Hard! I looked around and there stood a smiling man not much taller than me, saying "You just gonna look around, or you gonna shake my hand!" I simply smiled back, shook his hand, and moved on. He had a big smile and a hearty laugh. He had been the speaker that morning. I kind of liked him.

The Meetings Begin

When we showed up at the evangelistic series, I recognized the evangelist as the guy that thumped me. I was able to one-up my brother because I already "knew" the guy who is speaking! My brother was under-impressed with my social status, but then again, he was a teenager and was not impressed by much.

On the third night, as it neared time to get ready to go, my dad drove in from a long day's work. He had already pre-decided that he was going to have a headache that night and was going to opt out of attending the seminar. My mom said she was too tired to go also.

"Wait! We really wanted to hear tonight's topic!" My brother and I pleaded almost simultaneously.

What do you do when your kids say they want to go to church? You take them to church. We went that night, and we did not miss any nights after that.

The Call to Commit

One evening, as we approached the final week of the seminar, the evangelist gave a call at the end of the message. I had never seen a call before. I had no idea what was really going on. But what transpired around me that evening, rocked my world like never before.

As the organist played, the evangelist's wife sang and the evangelist looked at us. My mom began to sniffle, then it turned to actual tears and finally she sat there sobbing. My mom was never one to be quiet about anything. I sat there more embarrassed by the noise and commotion my mom was making and confused about what was going on, than noting what the speaker was doing. I was totally lost as to the implications of what I saw.

In my mom's words, she said, "I knew this message to be true. I had always believed it. Yet, I knew it meant that this would be a major life-change for us, for me. I knew that my husband was not going to go up front for the call with me. I did not know if I could do it alone. Thus, I began to cry. I was being called by Jesus. I was falling in love with Jesus. But I didn't know if I could do it alone."

We were sitting on the second row and making a scene, the likes of which I had never witnessed. We were all staring at the floor.

Again, in my mom's words, "I couldn't do this on my own, but I couldn't ignore Jesus either. I finally knew I had to go even if it meant going to church for the rest of my life by myself. I jumped up to go and my husband who had been resting his leg against mine, grabbed my hand. I thought he was trying to stop me, but instead, he was also on his feet too! My tears of fears were now transformed and pouring down my face as tears of joy!"

My brother and I looked at each other and I mouthed to my brother, "Where did they go? What's going on?" He simply said, "Shhh!" We both looked up at my parents who were hugging the evangelist. Then he turns to us and motioned for us to come up and join our parents. We did.

Honestly, I went home a little confused. But when I asked my parents on the way home what was going on, they said, "We've decided to join this church and begin going to church. We want us all to fall in love with Jesus." Cool! All that I had learned was amazing and I had learned that I too wanted to follow Jesus. Even though I did not know what the "call" was about, I was in total agreement.

The Transition

Thus, began a transition away from alcohol, working seven-days-a-week, living only for the sports in our lives. Our new life in Christ had begun. We soon learned to love the free Friday nights, as we would sit around the fire and read, eat popcorn and actually spend time together as a family. My dad discovered that in his construction company, he was able to accomplish more in six days, than he used to be able to do in seven. My parents were soon to discover that God could do more with the money they had left after tithe and offerings, then they used to get done with 100% of what they had.

We were baptized the next week in Cherry Creek, Oregon. The people at the swimming hole across the creek stopped to watch and observe. They were very polite. On the way to the last meeting of the seminar that evening, I leaned forward in the car and said to my family, "You know…if I'm going to be a Seventh-day Adventist Christian, I don't think I can play professional baseball anymore."

My parents were stunned. This was my dream. Most little boys want to become a baseball player one week, an astronaut the next, and a doctor the next. Not me. For as long as anyone could remember, I wanted to play professional baseball. It was my dream and I was working hard for that dream. I had never desired anything else, so they were stunned to see me say that. However, they were also stunned that I had come to that conclusion on my own. Evidently, I was going through my own conversion experience, not just following my parent's.

I sat back and let that sink in for a little bit. My parents were quiet, so was my brother. Then I leaned forward and pronounced, "If I can't play baseball...Maybe I'll be a preacher!" If my parents were stunned before, their jaws dropped to their laps with that amazing idea.

Today, I have spent close to 30 years in the ministry. This book talks about how I have made ministry work and why it works. It's the result of a conversion and learning to follow Jesus after first being introduced to him in an evangelistic series when I was just a 12-year-old boy. It's also the story of watching nearly 1,000 more people who were introduced to Jesus over the course of that ministry and seeing their lives changes, just like mine was so long ago.

2

Relevant Messages or Traditional? Really?

September 12, 2001, the day after the 9/11 attacks, my neighbor and I were standing in my yard talking about the previous day's events. He is a civil engineer and said, "Roger, what happened yesterday? We design buildings so they don't fall like that! I can't even put my mind around it. Does the Bible say anything about this kind of thing?"

This, of course, opened a whole lot of discussion that we had never had before. The idea of Bible and prophecy is huge in the wake of catastrophic events.

Someone once asked me why we use prophecy so much in our evangelism. My response was simple: Bible prophecy shows the Bible is truth. The whole reason most of our seminars start with Daniel 2 is not because it's such a powerful truth, but because it simply and effectively proves the Bible is true and can be trusted. When people see the timeline as it is played out in the metal image of Daniel 2, suddenly they have a reason to trust the Bible, that it speaks of truth before it happens. It gives the speaker credibility. It sets the stage for the rest of the seminar.

By using Daniel 2, we are answering objections before they even come up. There are people who show up at a seminar asking if the speaker can be trusted to speak truth. Yet, when we speak simply from the Bible without much extraneous interpreting, it says to the new person, "This seminar will focus on scripture and that can certainly be trusted."

When we set ourselves up as people who preach the Bible, we have a lot to stand on. The Bible does, in fact, fall on our side heavily on the things we teach and preach.

Once, a man came up to me during the seminar where I was not the speaker, and informed me, "I've been talking to my pastor about these things. I'm troubled by the Sabbath *(It could have been the State of the Dead; the literal, visible Second Coming; or any one of the other things which we hold dear)*. He's been looking at some scriptures with me and I want him to come talk with you. Would that be okay?"

He was trying to see if I would be willing to be set straight. Was I open to being corrected? His pastor was older, so must be obviously wiser in biblical knowledge than I. He thought his pastor would be able to rescue him from his growing conviction of the Sabbath. I believe he wanted to scare me about the upcoming meeting with his pastor.

My internal reaction was, "Bring it on baby!" What I said, was politer than that. I was not scared. I am very confident that the belief system which I hold is one of the strongest out there and is based solely on scripture. If you want to pit Adventism against any other denomination against us with the Bible as the guide, we win every time. The logic of our argument is clear.

I believe the "older, wiser" minister understood that. He never came. He never called. The Bible is on our side.

However, not everyone is interested in following the Bible as their main guide. One time a man said, "Pastor, you've shown me very clearly that the Bible Sabbath is Saturday. And when the Lord tells me to keep it, I will start doing so."

I sat there flabbergasted! After studying with this individual through the truths of the Sabbath, the Change of the Sabbath, through all of scripture. I stammered, "Where hasn't he shown you?" With my understanding of the Bible as the source of our guidance, I was surprised.

This individual went on to say, "When the Lord shows me, while I'm in the Spirit, then I'll know." He was simply saying, that unless the Sabbath was confirmed to him while he was speaking in tongues, he would not be keeping it.

I am convinced we need to do two things in evangelism. First, we must preach from the Bible. Evangelistic preaching, especially, is not a place to preach opinions, political divisions, or anything else. We must be a people of the Word of God. We must be a people of the Book!

Second, we must have a time where we introduce people to the distinctive things we teach. The Sabbath, the Second Coming, the State of the Dead, are all about the message of the gospel. They teach a truer picture of Christ and they show grace. The above story shows that there is so much deception abounding in the world. The truth we teach needs to be proclaimed somewhere and it needs to be shared with people who are confused and who need Jesus.

In his groundbreaking book, *"The Apocalyptic Vision and The Neutering of Adventism,"* George Knight clearly shows that when we move away from our theological roots and begin to be just like every other church out there, we will lose our doctrinal distinctives, we lose our heritage and we lose our relevance. Adventism has a prophetic purpose by which we must proclaim Jesus Christ. Knight says, "In the question-and-answer session that followed I made the point that if Adventism loses its apocalyptic vision, it has lost its reason for existing as either a church or as a system of education."[6] He is saying that our very existence depends on our preaching the message that we were raised up to preach. He continues, "As Seventh-day Adventists God does not call us to be prophets of respectability but proclaimers of the message of the Lion and the Lamb."[7]

According to Paul, there is a need for preaching the message. *"How then will they call on him in whom they have not believed? And how are they to believe in him of whom they have never heard? And how are they to hear without someone preaching?"*[8] So we must preach. People are waiting to hear.

I am not trying to discount the need to do caring ministries like feeding the homeless, teaching about health ministries, food

---

[6] Knight, G. R. (2008). *The Apocalyptic Vision and the Neutering of Adventism.* (G. Wheeler, Ed.) (p. 11). Hagerstown, MD: Review and Herald® Publishing Association.

[7] Knight, G. R. (2008). *The Apocalyptic Vision and the Neutering of Adventism.* (G. Wheeler, Ed.) (p. 25). Hagerstown, MD: Review and Herald® Publishing Association.

[8] The Holy Bible: English Standard Version. (2016). (Ro 10:14). Wheaton: Standard Bible Society.

banks, clothing ministries, or even simple friendship evangelism. Those are all good, and all churches should be involved in those and similar ministries. They are vital to the life of any church having a sense of living beyond themselves. Yet, these things are not what make us unique.

We have a treasure-trove of useful, life-changing information that does not change the gospel of grace, it only enhances it. People are desperately tired and in need of a rest. We have a huge piece of advice for them. That rest is not centered in the latest and greatest vacation, but in a Sabbath where they can reconnect to the Life-Giver who will give them not only restful sleep, but rest in their minds and rest in their very souls. The Sabbath is a message like no other. It is much needed in today's fast-paced world.

We are not arguing for the right day. We are arguing for time away to rest with our maker. This is a story of grace, that God wants to spend time with us.

When you view the Ten Commandments in Exodus 20, the reason for the Sabbath is a memorial for creation. When Moses repeats the Ten Commandments in Deuteronomy 5, it's in his last real message to the people before he hands the reigns over to Joshua. In Deuteronomy, he essentially repeats the Ten Commands word-for-word. Moses' only deviation from the word-for-word repetition is for the Sabbath commandment. That command is repeated nearly word-for-word itself, except for the reason to keep the commandment. In Exodus, we keep it as a memorial of creation. In Deuteronomy, we keep it as a memorial to redemption.

The Sabbath is a memorial of God's grace. It takes us from creation to redemption. Nothing else really presents us with such a good picture of the gospel. God wants to spend time with us – even us – the sinners! He wants to do it so much, that he redeems us. That is the gospel message like no other.

We have a tremendous message of hope. Hope is not in the next presidential election, it is not in the next piece of world-changing technology, it is not about any of those things. The hope we have is not found in politics, business or any other transient idea that comes along. Rather, our hope is in the second coming of Jesus Christ. There is no other fix that is as hope-filled or permanent.

Many people are walking around with no hope. In 2013, the suicide rates hit the highest in a quarter century.[9] People live in hopeless marriages. They are stuck in dead-end jobs. They distract themselves with sports, drugs, alcohol, sex and spending frenzies. These things are transient. However, the hope we have in Jesus Christ is extended to a future that is indescribably good. We have the best option available.

Our theology of the second coming is a message of hope. There is a hope beyond this world and it's coming soon!

My wife and I were giving a lady Bible studies early in our ministry. On the third or fourth study, near the end, this lady started telling a story about her mom. "My mom was the sweetest lady and I know she looks down and helps me through the problems of life. I miss her terribly, but I know she's watching and still helping me."

I simply nodded my head and listened. We went on with the study and when we got out to the car, my flabbergasted wife said, "Why didn't you tell her that wasn't true?"

"What wasn't true?" I had already forgotten about what the lady said about her mom in heaven.

"When she talked about her mom being in heaven. You just nodded your head and smiled as if you agreed with her!"

I explained that this lady was not ready to hear that truth yet. There is a reason Bible studies are presented in a certain order. New ideas take time to process. She would be ready to hear about what happens when we die, when we came to that topic, but until then, she would just close her mind to things that I was trying to get her to understand first.

I believe the doctrine of the state of death is one of our most hope-filled messages we preach. I know it's hard for people, emotionally, to move Aunt Mary out of heaven and back into the grave. Yet, think about the grace of this.

My wife and I have eight kids. If something horrible happened and my wife were killed in a car wreck, imagine what happens next. The common view, she goes to heaven and watches over me and her wonderful offspring. Yet, push the story further, say I get remarried to the proverbial evil step-mother. She beats the kids, ridicules them, yells at them, and abuses them. My first wife is up in heaven watching all this? Is that heaven or hell for

---

[9] https://en.wikipedia.org/wiki/Suicide_in_the_United_States

her? Clearly the most grace-full thing to do is to allow her to rest in the grave.

Every funeral I have ever been called to do for non-members, the family has been sure their departed grandpa, dad, mom, or sister is in heaven. Every funeral, they talked the best about the departed loved one, all except one.

I was called by the local funeral home to do a funeral for a family that did not have a church. I showed up on their doorstep to comfort them, give them some courage and to learn about the deceased grandfather so I could say something meaningful at the funeral service.

"Tell me about your grandfather/dad." I started.

"Oh, he was an evil man! He was horrible!" they all said in unison.

"Why do you say that?" I inquired, as I looked around at his pictures, his ornate carvings and his large extended family.

The family deadpanned. They did not know how to explain it. Finally, one of them informed me – and they were not telling me a joke, "We know he's burning in hell right now. No doubt about it."

I scanned the room, and everyone had a serious look on their face and were nodding their heads in agreement. That was an interesting funeral, for sure.

The message of what happens to you when you die is a message of grace for those who have family who are not headed to heaven. It's a message that makes more sense and gives a picture of God that is not vengeful, but hopeful and grace-filled.

The messages we preach are not old-fashioned with no relevance to people's lives today. In fact, they are just as relevant to life today as at any other time in history. The huge story of the Bible is that it is just as relevant today.

For example, John McVay writes, "at least fourteen of the twenty-two chapters [of Revelation] deal with worship."[10] One of the key reasons we spend so much time in Revelation is to call people out of false worship and call them into true worship. It's the Revelation of Jesus Christ. And preaching that message is vitally important to us as a people who want to make the Bible our standard and to help the community learn about the God we love and follow.

---

[10] http://www.adventistreview.org/1610-28

Evangelism Intelligence is about understanding why we do evangelism and how it really does preach the gospel of grace we love and desire to live by. It is part-and-parcel of the gospel. The message we preach not only is part of the gospel story, it's also what makes us unique.

The message of Revelation, the Revelation of Jesus Christ, is about much more than beasts, dragons and the like. Revelation is really more about Jesus and worshipping him than about anything else. It's a message that needs to be proclaimed to a world that is not worshipping Him.

This message of worship is a defining point for the Seventh-day Adventist Church. All three of the messages proclaimed by angels in Revelation 14 are centered in the topic of worship. Yet that message we preach needs to be relevant to people in today's world. Knight says we need to preach a traditional message from the 19th century, that is still relevant in the 21st.[11] I believe this is an obligation we hold.

The problem is, most churches today are taking an either/or approach. They are either going to be relevant or preach the 19th century message. This is what evangelism intelligence is about. The message is still true. Yet if it's not relevant, then it's of no value. It must be both/and, not either/or. Let's keep talking about how to do this.

---

[11] Knight, G. R. (2008). *The Apocalyptic Vision and the Neutering of Adventism*. (G. Wheeler, Ed.) (p. 88). Hagerstown, MD: Review and Herald® Publishing Association.

3

Adventist Churches Grow Differently

We were so excited! We had heard stories of churches launching on Easter and growing significantly. We were going to try it too. We knew we would experience amazing amounts of people checking out church again, on Easter. Most of the advertising we had seen from Outreach Marketing[12] was catchy, creative, according to the testimonies, it worked. The stories went something like this:

> *"We mailed out 5,000 postcards and on our opening week, we had 400 people show up. The next week we were down to 200, but within the first year, we had climbed back to 400 in our weekly attendance.[13]"*

The stories were always the same. Start with a splash and that big start will give you a close idea of what your attendance will be in one year. Understandably, we were pumped. We were a new church meeting in Greeley, Colorado. Our name was catchy, "The Adventure," and we had great music, casual feel, good preaching *(at least I thought so)* and already had a crowd of about 100 people attending.

---

[12] www.outreach.com
[13] This is a paraphrase of much of the testimonies we heard from Outreach marketing sales professionals and from their website.

We decided to do two services that upcoming Easter weekend. We wanted to be evangelistic, so we planned an epic Sabbath morning at our usual, rented facility and another on Easter Sunday, as an evangelistic event, in an auditorium at the local community college. We mailed out 10,000 eye-catching postcards that were painstakingly worded to draw a crowd. We prepared with our best music team, we had refreshments ready to go, and everything was spic and span for our incoming guests. As a church plant, we had prepped our language for our guests. We had taken the time to train people to be the best frontline greeters in the world and we were focused on reaching the lost.

Members began arriving early on Saturday morning. We prayed together, as usual. Our expectations were high. Surprisingly, not a single guest came. There were not even any Adventist guests that day. Our thoughts were, "Okay. Okay. This was Easter weekend. You can't expect the unchurched to come on Saturday." So, we prepped our ideas again for the next day. We prayed together more. We spruced up the message, the music and the food. This would be fun, new location, new people, and new growth for the kingdom. Same service, different location and plenty of excitement and help.

Everything was perfect for this service. It went off without a hitch…except we had only one visitor, and he came in 20 minutes late. We never saw him again. If this was what we expected our attendance to be like in one year, we were in a world of hurt. What went wrong?

The next day my family and I drove to Lincoln, Nebraska to meet with other church planters in middle America. I was exhausted and discouraged. I was heartsick and wondering if I had missed something in my prep work or our advertising choices. I was usually the "up" one at these meetings. Yet, I was down…waaa-aaay down. The preparation for the Easter weekend services had been exhausting. I needed some down time and recovery. We drove away from home with heavy hearts and plenty of doubt.

The church planters were top-notch people who wanted to do ministry with passion, excellence and be game-changers. This was the research and development team of the mid-America team of churches. They studied the books, went to the conferences and sent the postcards.

Sent out the postcards? Wait! When I began asking questions, I found out that nearly all of them, at various stages of their work, had also used similar postcards. Their results were similar or worse than mine. Why had I not known this before? Although the number of pastors (about 10) was small, the results were significant and telling. I was onto something, but I was not quite aware what yet.

I began to discuss this with a wider field of pastors whom I knew were trying their best to reach people for the kingdom. Some of them were church planters. Some pastored traditional churches. All were doing whatever they could to see Kingdom growth in their churches. As my friend Steven Shommler and I discussed it one day, he said, "I think I've got it figured out." His conclusions were arresting. I listened to his analysis.

Steven concluded, the people that respond to the postcard mailers are either 1) already churched and are looking for a new church to attend, or 2) formerly churched and are thinking about going back to church. They are looking for something familiar. Steven said, "Our worship on Saturday means they are not even considering us. They are not convinced of the Sabbath yet. They are all looking for a new church and everyone 'knows' churches meet on Sunday. Saturdays do not even come on their radar."

He was right. I knew it instinctively. I also knew it experientially. The testimonies at Outreach Marketing were correct, but none of them were from Adventists.

That began a process that said to me, *Adventist churches grow differently*.

Grow Differently?

What do I mean by Adventist Churches grow differently? Please let me explain. The church growth literature has many good ideas for helping a church to grow. As Adventists, we need to listen to and abide by much of that information as well. We still need to have a language people understand. We still need to run our services professionally and carefully with a sensitivity to the outsider visitor. We still need to be outreach minded. We can still learn a lot from other churches, and Ellen White affirms this when she talks about using methodology from non-Adventists to use in

teaching our kids in Sabbath school.[14] We are not talking about
learning theology or doctrine from others, but methodology. Their
methodology is not all wrong, and yet, it does not mesh
completely with Adventist churches.

Imagine this scenario with me. Mike and Sally wake up
one morning. Mike rolls over and says to Sally, "Wow honey! We
haven't been to church in years. What would you think about
going today?" Now, let me ask you. What day is it? It's Sunday, of
course. Nobody wakes up on a Saturday morning and says that,
except former Adventists. Most churches that worship on Sundays,
do not have to get people to cross a barrier to enter their services.
Sabbath is a wonderful thing, but it's a barrier for people to
overcome. I am not saying there is anything wrong with the
Sabbath. I am saying, Adventist churches grow differently.

Remember too, that we are not asking people for a couple
of hours of their week to attend church. We are asking people to
change what they do for 24 hours of each week of their life. The
whole world revolves around Saturday. It is the busy shopping
day, garage sale day, sports day and Sunday's are the day most
people relax. Worshipping on Saturday is a barrier to that lifestyle.
Adventists must use a different game plan for evangelism.
Adventist churches grow differently.

Another barrier comes in regard to finances. We are not
asking for an offering. Rather, we are asking for 10% tithe and 5-
10% offerings. When I hear from non-Adventist preachers, they
are amazed at how much Adventists give of their income. We are
not asking for them to give a simple offering; we are asking for a
major investment from their income to the kingdom. Adventist
churches grow differently.

When I say we grow differently, I believe our theology
demands it. When I was at Wayne Cordeiro's Leadership
Practicum[15], I met many non-Adventist ministers who said they
had changed denominations. When I asked them if the transition to
another denomination was hard, I continually heard back: "Not at
all. We all believe the same things. Some of the church polity was
different, but church is church."

---

[14] White, E. G. (1892). *Gospel Workers* (p. 324). Review and Herald
Publishing Association.
[15] www.enewhope.org

My response was thought-provoking for them, "Wow! For an Adventist to change denominations, you must change so much theologically. The Sabbath, death, second coming, prophecy, lifestyle issues…so much more are all different." To become an Adventist, you must assent not only to salvation in Christ and His grace upon you, but also to a new belief about what happens when you die, a different belief about the second coming of Christ, the Sabbath, diet related issues, the sanctuary, judgment, etc. Adventist churches grow differently. Our theology demands it.

The implication of Adventist churches growing differently is huge. The biggest thing that this means, is that it takes time to make a change to Adventism. People need time to contemplate the new ideas. They need time to make a proper decision because they have learned new truth. This answers one of the biggest complaints about evangelism: that it takes several weeks. However, when you think about changing your mind from a secret rapture to a visible, literal, audible second coming it takes time to process. When you think about accepting the Sabbath and changing the focus of your life so that it revolves differently from everyone else in your community, it takes time to process. When you have to move Aunt Betty from heaven back to the grave, it takes time to process. One of the reasons that evangelism takes three or more weeks is because it just takes time to process some of the life-change that must happen to become an Adventist Christian.

Suffice it to say that when you begin going to church in a non-Adventist church, you cross a spiritual barrier. You cross from unbelief to belief when you dedicate your life to Jesus. However, when you join an Adventist church, you not only cross that same spiritual barrier, you also cross a cultural barrier. The second coming requires a theological change. The state of death requires an emotional change and may be one of the hardest to get past. The Sabbath requires a life-style change. Clean and unclean foods require a dietary change. Potlucks are just different.

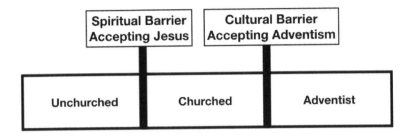

Figure 3-1: Spiritual and Cultural Barriers

Cultural Barrier Example: Potlucks are Different

A friend of mine, Robert, became an Adventist a few years before I met him, as a result of a Revelation Seminar he attended while a student at the University of Oregon. He later married Kari, a Baptist girl who would eventually become an Adventist, despite her first entrance into an Adventist Church.

Kari is not shy, and she easily made conversation with people as she came into church and they were invited to attend potluck. Kari's open and outgoing and immediately enthused, "Sure! I love church potlucks!"

As Robert and Kari worked their way through the potluck line, Kari talked occasionally with members in line, commiserated with Robert about food, and balanced her bread, plate and plastic ware, she looks at a dish on the table and says loud enough for the people around her to hear, "Is that fish?"

The people in the potluck line stopped dead in their tracks. Fish? No one knew what to say, until the little old lady behind her grabbed Kari's arm and said, "Oh honey, this is an Adventist potluck!"

Kari deadpanned. She did not understand the Adventists potlucks are usually vegetarian. She felt like a deer caught in the headlights. Insert uncomfortable silence, "So, is it fish?" she finally blurted again.

Evangelism Intelligence begins with this understanding: Adventist churches grow differently.

Adventist Churches Grow Differently

USA Today recently declared that Adventist Churches were the fastest growing church in North America.[16] There are several ways in which Adventist Churches grow. Two of those ways are having an Adventist hospital or an Adventist school nearby. Yet, the primary way which Adventist churches draw new members in, is through our public evangelistic efforts.[17] These are different than your average non-Adventist church.

Saying "Adventist churches grow differently" is not a downer. Not at all. But it helps us understand that our theology is different. We were raised up for something specific. If we become just another evangelical church that goes to church on Saturday, we will have lost our way. However, if we are the fastest growing, and evangelism is a big part of that, it only makes sense that we will pay attention to how to do it and to get better at doing it. Let's keep going.

---

[16] USA Today, March 17, 2011:
http://usatoday30.usatoday.com/news/religion/2011-03-18-Adventists_17_ST_N.htm

[17] Sahlin, M. (2008). Adventist Church Growth & Evangelism Research: Briefing for Presidents Council of the Pacific Union Conference (p. 37). Westlake Village, CA: Monte Sahlin Live Presentation.

4

Eight Myths of Evangelism

"What do you do for work, Aaron?" I broke ground to start getting to know Aaron as he had been coming to our seminar.

"Oh, I'm in business." His answer was vague, and I wondered why. The aloofness of his answer, made us wonder if he was really serious about the seminar.

Aaron and his wife Stacy had been attending our seminar since opening night. They were driving over 20 minutes each way to attend. They brought their two kids and came every night. At the end of each evening, they seemed in no hurry to get home. Aaron loved to engage the evangelist and me in questions, looking for understanding, etc. yet, when we asked if we could come visit him at his home, or at work, the answer was always no.

Unbeknownst to us, Aaron called his brother to talk about this incredible seminar where he was learning so much about the Bible. His brother, who had recently become a Seventh-day Adventist and had not shared it with any of his family, was concerned that Aaron may have wandered into some cult or something. However, he encouraged him to keep learning and to make sure the Bible is the true rule of thumb.

As we came near the end of the seminar, we still were not getting any response cards from Aaron and Stacy. So, my evangelist friend and I made an appointment with them to stay after the seminar one night. "Aaron, you've been here every night. What are you thinking about all we've been talking about here?" we asked.

Aaron let out a long sigh. "Okay, here goes…I believe what you are saying. I want to join your church, but I can't. I want to be baptized, but I can't…not yet anyway."

As we continued to question and push as to why he could not be baptized, Aaron went on to outline a complicated story that began with, "I own a strip club." Wait! Did he say a strip mall? No, he did not – our minds were racing now. No, this was the strip club that comes with the girls, alcohol, tips stuffed into skimpy clothing, etc. Aaron was not comfortable getting baptized until he had released his hands from it.

It took Aaron almost four years to get out of the family business. It was complicated by his dad's death and fighting for control with his step mom, and then with his brothers who wanted to stay in the business. He eventually was able to close the business, sell the building to a local church, and that now-closed strip club has become a church. Amazingly, that meant that the only strip club in Ft. Collins, Colorado was no more. There were no strip clubs in the city at all!

Today, I have a key to that old club. I carry it with me everywhere I go. It's a constant reminder to me that evangelism may change one life at a time, but it can also change a whole community just as quickly. Evangelism changes everything.

People have many different ideas about evangelism. Too many think things that are just outright wrong. They are myths.

I often refer people to the website www.snopes.com. It's a fabulous website that has made a name for itself as a truth checker for urban myths. Did the president really say…? Does peanut butter have rat hairs? What happened at the JFK Shooting? Who shot JR? So much information is appropriate in light of the many forwarded emails we get on a daily basis. Cute stories, evil stories, doctored pictures, etc. Snopes.com has it all and has become a reliable fact checker online.

I sometimes wish we had an AdventistSnopes.com to check the various Adventist myths about things that passed around via email, videos, church lobbies and pastors' meetings. In this chapter I hope to dispute some of the myths about evangelism. If we are really going to focus on Evangelism Intelligence, then the myths need to be addressed and documented as to why they are not true.

MYTH #1: Evangelism only teaches doctrine and does not present Jesus.

There are a number of problems in this statement. First and foremost, when I say, "Jesus is Lord," I have just expressed a doctrine that not everyone believes. When I say, "Our salvation comes because of the grace of God alone," I have expressed a doctrine. So, I am not sure how you could express any belief without expressing doctrines.

Doctrine, at it's very basics, simply means something that is taught. Doctrine is not necessarily a bad thing. I believe what the critics are really asking is, "Is our teaching formulated and based in Jesus, or simply based in theological argument?" This is a great question and one that needs to be answered. If our beliefs are not based on Jesus and only founded in a clear argument, we are not any different than the Pharisees of the Old Testament.

I believe that the more we know, the better we are able to understand God. I also believe that if our doctrine is not founded in Jesus and does not lead us to Jesus, then we are on the wrong track. Ellen White expressed, that "Of all professing Christians, Seventh-day Adventists should be foremost in uplifting Christ before the world."[18] Absolutely! If we are not centered on Christ, then where are we really going?

Yes, we do present quite a few theological arguments in our evangelistic meetings. However, frequently our new members say, "You've presented a fuller picture of Jesus to me!" Our doctrines are based on Jesus. The Sabbath is about spending time with Him. The state of the dead and hellfire is about God's mercy and grace and not burning people for eternity. The second coming is all about Jesus and salvation. I could go on, but you get the picture.

Doctrines are an important part of understanding Jesus. They are also an important part of understanding salvation. Doctrines make us unique and as the previous chapter expressed, Adventist churches grow differently, our theology demands it. I am not afraid of our doctrines, but they do need to be focused on Christ and Him crucified.

---

[18] White, E. G. (1915). *Gospel Workers* (p. 156). Review and Herald Publishing Association.

MYTH #2: Evangelism only turns active Christians into Adventists, it's not reaching the unchurched.

This myth comes out of the previous one that all we ever really teach is doctrine and people do not find Jesus at our meetings. The thinking is, true evangelism is about people finding salvation, not being convinced of right doctrine. It's only the "Metho-pisto-bapti-terians" who come, and then we teach them the Sabbath and they become Adventists. Yet, they were already convinced of Jesus. They were already walking with the Lord, right? We are not attracting the unchurched, right?

My personal study and documentation in this area, after being a part of more than 40 evangelistic events is that roughly 75% of the people who join our church after an evangelistic seminar come from an unchurched background. However, most unchurched people in America used to have some church in their background. According to ABC News, 83% of Americans still say they are Christian.[19] The New York Times reports more than 90% of Americans claim this, yet only about 40% nationwide actually attend church regularly, maybe less.[20]

I have had personal conversations with two previous directors of the North American Division Evangelism Institute.[21] Their numbers and mine are essentially the same. We are primarily baptizing unchurched people, not currently churched.

Our data has not always tracked churched vs. unchurched category. But when we added that data to our spreadsheet, we came up with these numbers: Most of the people we baptize are unchurched. Most of those in the already churched category leave. This is shown in Figure 4-1:

---

[19] See http://abcnews.go.com/US/story?id=90356&page=1

[20] http://www.nytimes.com/2014/05/18/upshot/americans-claim-to-attend-church-much-more-than-they-do.html

[21] From Personal Conversations with Russell Burrill and Ron Clouzet

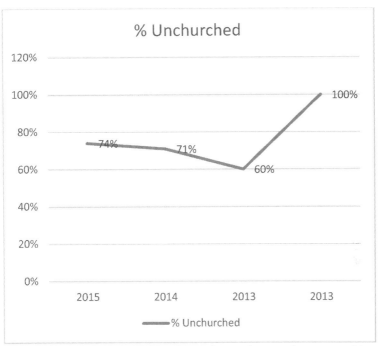

Figure 4-1: Most Recent Numbers, from when we began tracking churched category

Finally, according to Regele's book, *"Death of the Church,"* he says Seventh-day Adventists are very poor at stealing sheep.[22] A non-Adventist church-growth expert says that this myth is simply not true.

MYTH #3: No one Stays!

Joe said to me after church one day, "No one is here from the _____ seminar? Why do we even do these anymore?"

I said, "Sure there is! What about Bob? Dan? Susan?" "Oh, they were from those meetings?" I then rattled off another ten names while my friend stood there slack-jawed. Actually, I too walked away stunned. I was shocked that it was not as obvious to him as it was to me that the people really were still here.

---

[22] Regele, Mike, (1995) *Death of the Church* (p. 155) Zondervan Publishing

It was from that conversation that I started keeping a spreadsheet on evangelism. This spreadsheet covers a variety of things like how much it costs to bring a person through the front doors of the church ($210), how much does each baptism cost ($2400), the retention of people (70%), response rates for the brochures (2-3/1000) and a few other things.

From that spreadsheet, I have tracked every seminar my churches have done since 2001. The numbers say our long-term retention rate hovers around 70%.[23]

So, I started analyzing why people say "No one stayed after a year." I have talked to countless people and analyzed just as many conversations of members. Here is my take on the issue.

1. We are keeping 65-70% of the people we baptize. I have that much documented.
2. Of those that stay 70+% are from an unchurched category. I have that documented also.
3. The ones who leave, are primarily those that were active in another church already before they came to our meetings.
4. The ones who stay, get integrated into the life of the church very quickly.

That last point, that people get integrated into the life of the church, is key to this issue, I believe. We have discovered, the when new people are so excited about their church, they get involved quickly. After a year or two, the "old" members subconsciously think, "We couldn't do church without Bob and Jane, so they must have been here a long time." In other words, the new people get so integrated into the life of the church that they do not seem new anymore.

This seems to be the core message around people not staying. I am sure there are people who have a different experience. However, I like what one of my ministerial friends said, "People come to me and say 'We baptized ten people at the last seminar and no one from that seminar attends church anymore. Evangelism doesn't work.' I simply say, back to them, Wait! You said that ten people got baptized. It sounds like the evangelistic

---

[23] This is from a personal study of my own, but is also similar to the numbers I get from personal conversations with Ron Clouzet and Russell Burrill, former Directors of the NAD Evangelism Institute.

seminar did the job it was intended to do. Evangelism worked, but the church did not."[24] What did the church do about discipling people once they were brought in. That is a topic for a future book, I am sure.

It is true that people leave after evangelism. There are two general groups of people who leave. The first group is those who are tied into another church with family, friends, or service already. They come because they are interested in learning more about the Bible, going deeper. They are under conviction of the Sabbath or other ideas and they decide to join, but their attachment is so strong with the other church that they soon drift back. What I have found is that most of the people we lose within the first year, were strongly attached to their previous church. This, again, seems to back up Regele when he says we are not good at getting people from other churches. It is simply hard to get people to break away from their social and emotional support of their church.

The second group of people who leave within the first year, are people that are already members of our churches. We have found that every time we do an evangelistic series and bring in new people, some members who were already here at our church, who were on the fringe, leave. Some of them go to another church, some of them drop out of church altogether. However, this is not a problem with evangelism. This, again, is a problem with discipleship. I do believe this is more pervasive than just my churches. The people, within the Adventist Church who are on the fringe, are very close to leaving. Again, this is not a problem with evangelism, but of discipleship and congregational care.

Sure, there are unchurched people who leave after joining. But that is not the norm. That is not a major problem in our evangelism across the NAD.[25] The chart below shows our retention over the last 6 years averages out to 71%. The previous 8 year's retention rate was at 66%.

Here are my statistics:

---

[24] From a conversation in the Evangelism Committee of the Oregon Conference.
[25] Sahlin, M. (2008). Adventist Church Growth & Evangelism Research: Briefing for Presidents Council of the Pacific Union Conference (p. 26). Westlake Village, CA: Monte Sahlin Live Presentation.

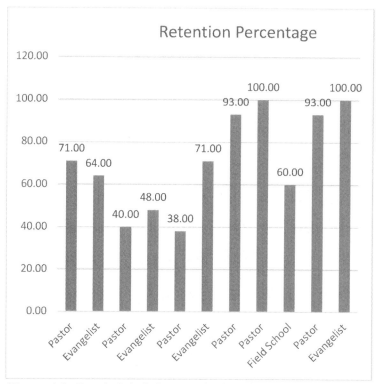

Figure 4-2: Simply labeled as to whether the local pastor or a hired evangelist did the seminar

MYTH #4: The only people who attend evangelistic meetings are the Retired, Unemployed or Socially Unique

This myth comes from the idea that the only people who can afford the time to attend meetings five nights a week for 3-5 weeks are those who do not have a day-job or who are simply weird. It's the idea that no normal person can afford that kind of time away from their TVs, Facebook cat videos or their families.

My only answer to this would be to walk you through my list of names we have baptized as a result of our evangelism. People holding good jobs, in their 30s, who had kids and came night-by-night. I can show you that the names and number of people who come and show that the majority of people we have baptized have been young families through our evangelism.

Mike and Sara were my neighbors. We had spent some time with them and other friends and were just getting to know them. One day, about a week before the seminar, we were all together and I simply asked them, "Did you see the prophecy seminar that is coming to Greeley?" Mike and Sara seemed genuinely interested in coming. They were in their young 40s and had five kids. Even though it was about a 20-minute drive, they came every night and brought their tribe with them each night.

My statistics show that the average age of those people we are baptizing is approximately 42. Monte Sahlin says the average age for new members is 44.[26] Yet, within the Adventist church, there are twice the percentage of people over the age of 50 than the general population.[27] The Adventist church is aging faster than the population around us.[28] There only two ways to keep it young – having more children or doing more evangelism!

What we have found is that meeting times that begin at 7:00 or 7:30 pm are getting too late for the school week and for people to bring their kids night-by-night. We have experimented with meetings beginning as early as 5:15 pm, 6:00pm, and 6:30pm. Lately, we have kind of settled on around beginning at 6:00 or 6:30 pm with a simple, hour-long program. We have discovered with these earlier time slots that a younger crowd comes out.

First, the early time gets people home at a decent hour to put their kids to bed. If they go home first, it's harder to get them out for a late night (for their kids) meeting. We are also finding that people eat afterwards if we are done by 7:00 or 7:15 pm. The earlier time slot gets them home in time for their family.

Second, the early time slots actually bring out more of our unchurched crowd. We have seen this time and again, where more non-Adventists, more unchurched come to the early time slot,

---

[26]Sahlin, M. (2008). *Adventist Church Growth & Evangelism Research: Briefing for Presidents Council of the Pacific Union Conference* (p. 27). Westlake Village, CA: Monte Sahlin Live Presentation.

[27] Sahlin, M. (2003). *Adventist Congregations Today* (p. 29). Lincoln, NE; Nampa, ID: Center for Creative Ministry; Pacific Press.

[28] Sahlin, M. (2007). *Adventists in North America—A Situation Estimate*. Riverside, CA: Adventist Today.

more members to the later. The earlier time slots are disliked more by the members and volunteers at the meetings. There is a fine balance to play between keeping your volunteers happy and getting more new people to come. However, I usually land on the side of more unchurched. So, we have kind of settled on starting around 6:00 pm or 6:30 pm and ending 60-75 minutes later.

In the end, when the four to five nights a week are over, the members go "Whew!" And the new people are saying, "What am I going to do with my time now?" The new people love what they are learning for the first time and want to continue to come 2-3-4 nights a week. They are not missing their TVs, they are not missing Facebook. They want to keep learning and keep coming. This is where follow-up is important and we will discuss that later.

We have found they aren't socially unique, retired or unemployed. It's a myth.

MYTH #5: Evangelism costs too much!

Now, it is true, mailing brochures, bringing in an evangelist, and doing an evangelistic series is expensive. Yet, it is not nearly as expensive as you might think. What we have found, dollar-for-dollar, evangelism is the cheapest, least expensive and most effective thing we have done to bring new members into the church. Around North American Adventism, it's costing around $5,000-7,000 per baptism.[29] As I look at my spreadsheet we are spending about $2,400 per baptism. Even Monte Sahlin's numbers back this up, our most effective means of bringing new people to the church is through our direct mail brochures.[30]

My church in Colorado spent roughly 40% of their monthly budget on outreach. We tried all kinds of things to bring people to church: seeker services, small groups, kindness projects, outreach softball, and many, many creative outreach projects,

---

[29] Joe Kidder's Numbers are significantly different when you factor in all costs of running the church/denomination vs. all new members. The combined numbers are $42,000/baptism in 2010 vs. $8,000 in 1948. See https://www.ministrymagazine.org/archive/2011/02/the-long-view-of-church-growth.html

[30] Sahlin, M. (2008). Adventist Church Growth & Evangelism Research: Briefing for Presidents Council of the Pacific Union Conference (p. 19). Westlake Village, CA: Monte Sahlin Live Presentation.

community service, events, speakers, etc. What we found is that dollar-for-dollar evangelistic seminars were the most cost-effective thing we did.

Lately we have been experimenting with other, less expensive forms of advertising: online, Facebook, yard signs, etc. Those other ways are so cheap, and certainly must work, right? We have found that those only back-up the mailed brochure. I must admit, Facebook is interesting. You can save a lot of money and really hand-pick your target audience by choosing age, ethnicity, income level, and even location. Yet, in our recent trials, we have found that even though 5,000 people click on and look at our ad, no one – literally no one – is coming out. Our conclusion is two-fold. First, Facebook advertising may work for online places where people can click on the ad, go to the website and buy something from the website, but lately, that is even being questioned by the experts. However, it's certainly not working when it requires people to move away from their computers, get into a car, drive to an unfamiliar location and attend a series of meetings. Second, if it's backing up a brochure that has been put in the mail, it's inexpensive and may help some as a reminder of the brochure people have on their kitchen counter.

People are really beginning to question online advertising and are coming to the conclusion that the direct-mail campaigns are still reaping better rewards. One article suggests that direct mail advertising is 34 times more effective than email for return on investment.[31] Here is a list of articles that discuss the issues pertaining to this:

- http://www.theatlantic.com/business/archive/2014/06/a-dangerous-question-does-internet-advertising-work-at-all/372704/
- http://smallbusiness.chron.com/average-rate-return-direct-mail-campaign-23974.html
- http://www.mccarthyandking.com/direct-marketing-tutorials/learning-direct-mail-response-rates
- https://www.onlinemarketinginstitute.org/blog/2013/06/why-direct-mail-still-yields-the-lowest-cost-per-lead-and-highest-conversion-rate/

---

[31] http://printinthemix.com/Fastfacts/Show/575

Now, let me say something more about the cost. When I moved to Colorado, I asked my Ministerial Director if I could have $8,000 for evangelism. He nearly choked, and his eyes popped out when I mentioned that sum. They had never given anyone that much money for evangelism before. Yet, because he wanted to support this new evangelistically focused church plant, they gave it to us. What he did not know then, and was going to find out later, was that I was going to ask for more the next year, and more after that.

Almost everything has gone up in price over the years. Everything that is except what we are willing to pay for evangelism.

To illustrate, I gave a testimony at a church in Michigan. During the potluck lunch afterwards, a guy came and ate with me. He said, "We started our church the same time you started yours. Our church only has 35 people coming. Yours has 250. Why? What's different?"

I began to tell him about the value of outreach and evangelism. However, his immediate response was, "We tried evangelism, that doesn't work anymore."

I probed a little deeper, "How much did you spend on your last evangelistic seminar?" His answer was $5,000. "That's why your evangelism isn't working," I shared with him. "I wouldn't even bother to do evangelism unless I could spend at least $25,000 and I've spent upwards of $60,000. You can't even draw a crowd with $5,000." Public evangelism is one ministry that is meaningfully benefitted by significant increases in resources.[32]

Sadly, this gentleman walked away not believing what I was saying. It makes sense to ask questions of people who are ahead of you in whatever game you play. It makes sense to ask someone questions who is better at something than you. It makes sense to seek out more information. Yet, whenever I seek out someone more knowledgeable to ask questions, I do not argue with the person about why their idea is stupid, rather I take notes on what they are saying. I do not think I will ever understand why people do this.

---

[32] Sahlin, M. (2007). *Adventists in North America—A Situation Estimate*. Riverside, CA: Adventist Today.

Everything costs more these days. My parent's first house cost about $8,000 in 1958. My first house cost $60,000 in 1991. Today the average house is over $250,000. Cars cost a lot more, so do staple food items. Everything costs more today than it did in 1950. You know all that, so why am I telling it to you now?

You cannot spend for evangelism like it is 1950 in 2017 and expect to get the same results we got in in 1950. I tell my conference president all the time, "I'm the only Anglo church keeping up with the Hispanic Churches on baptisms."[33] Why? Partly because we, as a church, have been willing to invest what it takes to make it work. I will not spend less than $30,000 anymore. It just does not work.

My good friend Hiram Rester likes to say that "a 1957 Chevy retailed for $2,800. A 2018 Chevy Camaro costs about $30,000. We have always been able to do evangelism for the price of a new car!" He's absolutely correct.

When the NAD Evangelism Institute[34] came to do a Field School in Loveland Colorado, Russell Burrill called in the seven area pastors who would be helping conduct the seminar. He presented his budget, it was in the neighborhood of $75,000. While all the other pastors gulped and began to wonder and sweat about how it was going to affect their church's budget, I raised my hand and said, "That budget is not large enough!"

Russell's jaw dropped clear to his knees. He asked me what I meant. I told him, "Do the math. Spend $75,000 and we're going to get 30 baptisms. That is awesome. But when you divide that by seven churches, that means everyone walks home with three or four new people. I am not trying to belittle that effort. There is much to be applauded for that. However, bringing all seven churches together is a BIG deal. You are bringing in 25 students to learn that evangelism works and with that you want to have the various churches go home thinking their effort was worth it. We want to have a bigger harvest for all this work."

As I was talking, the other pastors were listening and beginning to nod their heads. They were catching the vision and

---

[33] In a three year average, my church was the only Anglo church in the top ten, and we were number two on the list. Plus we took a year off from evangelism in one of those years.

[34] North American Division Evangelism Institute, based in Berrien Springs, MI.

forgetting about their bottom line budget for a moment. Russell exclaimed, "I've never had a pastor say my budget was too small before." When he returned, he had a budget of $100,000. The next time it was $125,000. We eventually lifted his budget to over $200,000 and baptized 90 people in that series. That was a cost of $2,200 per baptism.

Evangelism does not cost too much. It does cost, and we need to be willing to pay that cost for the kingdom growth we want to see. We pay our ministers more today, we pay more for buildings, we pay more to do our worship services, our kids programming, etc. Why not pay the right amount to get the crowd, to get the results in our evangelism?

Evangelism Intelligence means that if you are not willing to spend the money, stop saying it does not work.

MYTH #6: Evangelism interrupts the life of the church

Okay, this one may actually be true in a lot of churches. Church is going along smoothly. Then about every three years or so, everything stops in order to do evangelism. After it is over, church life returns to "normal." Evangelism becomes an interruption.

Churches that do not integrate the life of the church around the constant theme of reaching lost people do find this to be true. However, is that the way it should be? What if we integrated evangelism into the church schedule and made it a part of the process, not an interruption.

For us, we have a yearly cycle in our church. It is illustrated in Figure 4-3.

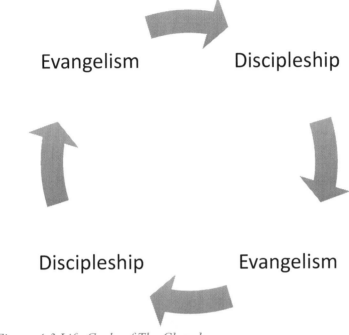

Evangelism   Discipleship

Discipleship   Evangelism

Figure 4-3 Life-Cycle of The Church

The idea behind this, is that we lead up to evangelism with discipleship and prep work. Which naturally flows into the discipleship and back into evangelism. In other words, the life-cycle of the church ebbs and flows around evangelism and discipleship. Both are valid and important. If a church only focuses on discipleship, they soon become ingrown. If they only focus on evangelism, they become tired and less full themselves. Both are important.

The real myth is that we do church without regularly integrating evangelism into "normal." Why is it okay that churches can go along for years without ever reaching lost people as part of their plan of ministry? The Great Commission is to GO, not stay in our own little holy huddle. The myth is really that churches that do not reach out are okay.

Evangelism ought to be part of the process and cycle of the yearly schedule, not an interruption to the life of the church. If we planned for it, if all our events lead up to it, this one would not be true. Unfortunately, this myth is too often not a myth.

MYTH #7: Evangelism does not work in today's world

The theory behind this myth is that people have changed over the years. Evangelism worked, supposedly, with the WWII generation, but not in today's postmodern world. It's only the retired, unemployed, or socially unique who still come *(see above, Myth #4)*.

Jim and Jerri came to our seminar in Sweet Home, Oregon. They came and introduced themselves to me the first night. Jim and Jerri came every night and were baptized at the end of the seminar. Turns out, during the course of the seminar, Jim quit smoking. As we got to know them, we found out that they babysat for some close friends of ours. Our friend was troubled by Jim and Jerri's decision. She was even more troubled by his quitting smoking. You see, Lisa had talked herself into believing that religion was no longer valid and no longer of anyone's personal interest. Then the people watching her kids are so changed, she struggled with understanding and coming to grips with her philosophy of life.

Basically, what people are saying with this myth is that people no longer have an innate desire to know truth at its core anymore. To a large degree, that is true. We live in a world of relativity these days. That means people say, "What's right for you isn't right for me. Truth is relative. Truth is whatever you mean, or I mean for it to be. It might be different for you. It might be different for me. That's okay. Truth is relative, there are no absolutes."

However, what we are finding out is that there are about 7% of the population in the U.S.A. that has a biblical worldview, part of which says there is a moral, absolute truth, found in the Bible.[35] You can find this in Figure 4-4. Only about 4% of people actually say they would be interested in attending a seminar to

---

[35] https://www.barna.com/research/barna-survey-examines-changes-in-worldview-among-christians-over-the-past-13-years/

learn more about the Bible.[36] These are primarily the people we reach, those who already believe the Bible, and want to know more about it. Monte Sahlin points out that that four out of five new members say that the "truth and beauty" of what we teach is what attracted them.[37] They want to know and understand more. Shane Anderson says that the "unique beliefs of the Adventist Church are immensely compelling to many people.[38] This small crowd believes there may still be an absolute truth. These are the people who come to our prophecy seminars. These are the people that we have reached within Adventism. On a broad scale, it's what most of Christianity has reached as well. There are pockets of the other 90% being reached, but nothing consistently and nothing that seems to be reproducible from place to place.

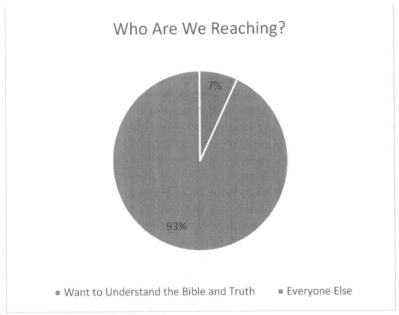

Figure 4-4: Worldview Percentage

---

[36] Gladden, R. (2003). *The 7 Habits of Highly Ineffective Churches* (p. 49). Lincoln, NE, AdventSource

[37] Sahlin, M., & Richardson, P. (2002). *Converts to the Adventist Church* (p. v). Milton Freewater, OR: Center for Creative Ministry.

[38] https://www.ministrymagazine.org/archive/2014/02/learning-about-evangelism

I understand that 7% is not much of society, yet in my community, that translates into 8,000-12,000 people that are open to hearing more. We have barely begun to reach that portion of society. Yet, in the last six years, my church baptized 220 people who are active and vital to our ministry. This has made us one of the fastest growing churches in North American Adventism.

I understand that 7% is not much in the overall scheme of people, yet when I Pastored two churches in Lebanon and Sweet Home, Oregon, in a town of 30,000 and 12,000 respectively, we took those two churches from 80 and 40 respectively to 185 and 75 in attendance in a matter of six years. In one year alone, we saw 96 people join our church.

I understand that 7% is not much of the population base, yet when we church planted in Colorado at a church called The Adventure, we grew that church from four families at the beginning to over 400 in monthly attendance and 250 on a weekly basis. We baptized about 60 people per year. This made us one of the ten fastest growing churches in the NAD.

My point? 7% does not sound like very many people, but there are still quite a few people to reach. We must get busy reaching them.

According to Shane Anderson, nothing works as well to commit people to Christ as a full-message series.[39] Even if evangelism only reaches 7% of the population, do not stop, just figure out how to reach those in the 7% at least.

Two small, traditional churches. A contemporary church plant. A large metropolitan church with a blended worship style, all have been some of the fastest growing churches because of using traditional evangelism, by primarily reaching the small 7-10% of the population.

Evangelism still works, when done properly. There are plenty of people to reach. True, it does not reach every segment of our society, but we can sure capitalize on where it does.

Evangelism Intelligence means though, that we need to understand who we are reaching. We will cover that in our next chapter.

---

[39] https://www.ministrymagazine.org/archive/2014/02/learning-about-evangelism

Ron brought his wife Crystal to our seminar. However, about half-way through the seminar, we learned that they were not married. They used to be married but had been divorced for over two years. When Ron received the brochure in the mail, he called Crystal and invited her to attend with him.

At the end of the seminar, we baptized them in church and at the end of the church service, we did a surprise wedding for the congregation as well. God brought these two people – in their mid 40s – to the kingdom and healed a very broken relationship.

Evangelism certainly does still work in today's world.

Myth #8: We need more compassion ministries, not another seminar

This myth is saying lifestyle evangelism, or compassion ministries and hope ministries are of a great importance. This is about the idea that we must show the world that we are Christians. It's similar to the idea that you should never have to preach, but simply "live the Christian life" and people will somehow come flocking to church. It is defined as kindness evangelism, friendship evangelism, community services center, God's Closet, food pantries, clothing banks, etc.

There are several problems with this. First, these ministries are definitely necessary. We do need to walk-the-walk, not just talk-the-talk. We need to be serving the community, helping and providing compassion ministry in our cities. No doubt about it. However, these ministries are not primarily set up to bring people to the point of decision. That is what our traditional evangelistic seminars are designed to do. They must go hand in glove together. If you only have the preaching and no compassion or healing ministries, you are preaching heartless truth. If you only provide help, hope, compassion and never get around to preaching, you are not giving the full message of what the Adventist Church was raised up to preach.

Second, if we never preach, we are ignoring what Paul calls the foolishness of preaching.[40] Further, Paul clearly says that

---

[40] See 1 Corinthians 1:21

some will never hear unless we preach and the preaching is beautiful.[41]

Please hear what I am saying, we definitely need ministries of compassion, hope and healing. Those are vitally important to the Christian process of reaching lost people, but these must also be accompanied at some point in the year by the message of preaching. George Knight says, "Thus, while He continued to feed the poor and point out the need for social justice, *Jesus' principal focus was the "irrelevant" one of the radical cross and the preaching of the gospel of full redemption from a world of sin.*"[42]

Daniel and Jessica did not receive a brochure in the mail from us, because they did not have an address. They lived on a boat on the Columbia River. They were homeless. They came, because one of my members was walking down the street, while he was talking on the phone. As he passed them, he did not break stride or stop his phone call, but he handed them a brochure. My friend looked at them, nodded, and kept walking. Daniel and Jessica did not recognize my friend until almost the last night of the seminar. When they saw each other, they embraced in a bear hug and Daniel just kept saying, "Thank you for giving me that brochure! Thank you!" That is when I heard the whole story. During the course of the seminar, we were able to get them an abundance of food, clothing, a DVD player and many other useful and needed items of compassion. They came night-by-night and we later married them and baptized them.

People who say it does not work in today's world, either are not doing it by the book (See Chapter 5), or they are not spending enough money to get it done (see Myth #5 above). Our church definitely does need compassion, hope, healing and preaching to work hand-in-hand for success.

For now, these are some of the most prevalent myths in evangelism. They don't stack up to reality, but they are prevalent in today's Adventist culture. My hope is that what this chapter

---

[41] See Romans 10:14-15

[42] Knight, G. R. (2008). *The Apocalyptic Vision and the Neutering of Adventism.* (G. Wheeler, Ed.) (p. 99). Hagerstown, MD: Review and Herald® Publishing Association. *(emphasis his)*

addresses will be told far and wide, so we can quit talking about why evangelism doesn't work. Instead, we should simply get out and get involved in evangelism.

5

Why Evangelism Works

"I want to get baptized!" exclaimed Vince on opening night of the seminar.

"Great! Let's sit down and talk sometime and schedule something towards the end of the seminar." I replied. I *KNEW* no one was ready to become a member and get baptized on opening night. What I learned through the seminar, seemed to confirm this conclusion.

You see, Vince had come from a family that struggled with drug abuse. As an adult, he had been a drug user and alcohol abuser. Unbeknownst to me, Vince had recently had a personal conversion experience. He had been reading his Bible and come to understand the Bible Sabbath and some of the other truths unique to us. At the end of the seminar, Vince, His wife Sharon and their two kids were some of the first of the 43 people we baptized that night. Vince still gives me a hard time for my original answer.

Vince owned a struggling construction business. After his conversion, it began to thrive. That prosperity came because Vince was moving out of the chaos of his life and into some solid ideas to live by. He was not using drugs anymore. He had stopped drinking. These two things alone, made his financial picture better on their own. However, Vince started showing up for work on time, working all day, and he did his work without the fog he used to live in, and his work became some of the best work in town.

Vince's crew used to laugh at him. When I would come to see him on the job site, they would point to his pickup. Vince would be sitting on the tailgate giving a subcontractor, cement truck driver, or a salesman a Bible study. He was sharing his faith more than he was pouring concrete!

Vince later moved to a smaller town in Oregon with the goal of relocating his vocational concrete business to support his avocation of starting a new church. Vince successfully planted that church, built them a building and later moved to another town where he is now planting a second church. He takes two or three weeks off every summer, in the busiest time in the construction industry, so he can volunteer for the maintenance and security department at the Oregon camp meeting. He always has a smile and you can usually find him talking about Jesus and letting some of the maintenance items wait.

Evangelism not only changes lives, it also changes communities. Why does it work?

Adventism has primarily worked in the middle to lower middle-class demographics of our society. What is amazing is that once people come into our ranks, their socioeconomic status raises. Why?

- We give them a quality educational system.
- We teach them to take care of their bodies and get off junk food, alcohol and cigarettes. This saves their body and their money at the supermarket and the doctor's office.
- We teach them how to manage their finances through our tithe and offering emphasis.
- We get them serving others.

There are some rather significant principles that make evangelism work in today's world. It's about more than the amount of money raised, it's about more than the focus of the church, and it's about the type of people that we are trying to reach.

From Chaos to Life-Integration

Let me focus in on one area for a moment. It's been shown that people in life-change move through a pattern of growth like the chart below:[43]

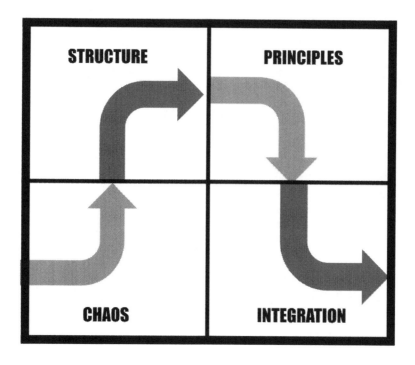

Figure 5-1: Life-Change Matrix

This chart is a generalization about how people work through life-change. In 1967, Holmes and Rahe studied 5,000 medical patients and came up with their stress scale.[44] Figure 5-1

---

[43] This chart was drawn by me, after a presentation/conversation with Jim Brauer around 2008. It came from his recollection of a class he took in the early 1980s at Andrews University.

[44] For a more complete list of the Holmes and Rahe Stress Scale, see: https://en.wikipedia.org/wiki/Holmes_and_Rahe_stress_scale. You can

above, demonstrates most people enter life-change because of some form of chaos: death of a spouse, change of career, move homes, distrust of a system, illness, loss of work, poverty or simply that the current system they live in is not working. It's Chaos. Monte Sahlin, in 2008, showed us some of these same issues leading up to a person's conversion and becoming an Adventist.[45] Life-change affects us all.

When people realize that their life is in chaos and they need change, they usually turn to some structure, some system, some way to understand and then change where they are headed. When they realize their weight has become unmanageable (chaos) they turn to a diet (structure). When their finances are out of whack (chaos) they turn to a budget and get financial help (structure). When they come to a church for the first time in years, it's usually some form of chaos that has hit their life, and they want some relief from it. This is represented in the chart turning up to structure. It's not a direct, straight path. This new structure involves change. Moving from chaos to structure is always an uphill battle, thus the chart turns up. It's not easy, but it is good.

This change might involve a new way of living, a new understanding of life. It may be as simple as beginning to hang up your clothes at night because you are tired of the chaos of the closet. It could be as large as changing the day of worship because of a new structure you have needed in your life.

Chaos dominates so many people's lives. Their marriages are falling apart, they hate their job, they are too disorganized, someone in their family is very sick, or has recently died. Chaos could come in the form of moving across town, or across the country for a new job opportunity, or even in retirement. The era for employment for life is over. Most people change careers three to seven times in their life.[46] All of these play into the concept of living in chaos. They also help people get ready for change.

---

take the test at this site:
https://www.mindtools.com/pages/article/newTCS_82.htm
[45] Sahlin, M. (2008). Adventist Church Growth & Evangelism Research: Briefing for Presidents Council of the Pacific Union Conference (p. 40). Westlake Village, CA: Monte Sahlin Live Presentation.
[46] https://www.thebalance.com/how-often-do-people-change-careers-3969407

When people get tired of the chaos, they usually turn to some form of structure to help them. Initially, the structure is your life. A person lives by that structure because it's the right thing to do. It works in my life. I have followed simple reminder lists and counted the days I have succeeded for years. It is a structure. I track my daily walk with a GPS on my iPhone® and have measured it monthly and yearly for years now. It is a structure that keeps me from getting lazy. I used to do it because it helped motivate me. Now I just continue to keep track, because it is simply what I do.

Over time, the principles get incorporated into a person's life and people then follow not only because they were told they were good, or simply because they need a motivator, but they come to understand that the structures are right for them. They can see the structure making huge changes in their lives. They can see the good that comes to them by walking away from chaos and moving into the structure. They analyzed that structure and figured out why it works for them. They begin to live on the principles. They no longer make the changes because they are in chaos. Now they keep the structures because the principles are right and for them make sense. The structure is still there, but it is not the motivator. They are living by principle now.

Over still more time, people tend to integrate all of this into the very fabric of who they are. Sometimes they cannot fully explain why they do things, but it is part and parcel of who they are and how they live. When others look at these people, they no longer see someone who does these things, they see someone who IS these things.

How does this relate to Evangelism? The 7-10% of the people who are open to learning more about the Bible (that we talked about in the last chapter) are not all ready to hear what we teach. They may come for a few nights to evangelistic meetings, but they generally see a few things they like, learn a few things and move on. The people we tend to "catch" in evangelism are those who live currently in some form of chaos or another.

I am going to generalize here, however it's not all inclusive. I could show a few examples of breaking the ideas about to be presented. Yet, in general, this works so much more of the time that you can see the trend easily when it happens.

The people we tend to reach in evangelism are in the middle-income or lower middle-income bracket. They haven't arrived financially. They usually have more month than money at the end of each paycheck. They are struggling in their finances, their marriage, their parenting or in their health.

Often people are in a major life-change. Someone significant has died, someone has lost a job, there has been a major move across the country, kids are going to school, kids have left home, their marriage is on the rocks or any number of the stress things that happen in life like death, disease, or major life-change.

My friend Richard Halverson tells a story of Doris and Bob. They were only living together, while they waited for the divorce papers to come in the mail they could sign them and move on with their lives, separately. The day their divorce papers arrived, they also found a brochure inviting them to a seminar Richard was conducting in their city.

They both wanted to go and decided to go…together. They figured they could sign the divorce papers later. What they saw was a something incredible about Jesus, about a way to change their lives. They attended, together, every night and were later baptized. Doris and Bob tore up their divorce papers and became active in a structure of church that continues.

We underestimate the amount of chaos in people's lives. Most people have some form of chaos in their life. That chaos could be simply a longing for God or deeper learning about him. When people get a brochure in the mail and are already open to learning more about what the Bible says – the 7-10% – they schedule themselves to come. About night number two or three they learn that this seminar will last longer, and they are not so sure anymore. However, they had scheduled the time, so they continue to come for the 5 nights in the brochure.

Ron was like that. He came out to a seminar in Greeley, Colorado and told me, "I do not have enough time to come to these. I am not coming for the next 4 weeks!" The speaker had just announced on night number 2 that this seminar would last four weeks. Then on night number 4, Ron came out and found me again and said, "Okay, I'm hooked. I'm coming to every one of these." Ron did come to every night. We baptized him, his wife, and his adult daughter.

The reason our evangelism works is that people are 1) interested in the Bible and 2) they see a structure to help them out of their chaos. When we present our evangelistic seminars, it is aimed directly at this group of people. It's why we use the brochures we use. It's why we use the order of messages we use. These are all part of the structure we present.

After a year or two, the average new person has come out of chaos and has been living in a world of right/wrong structure. The structure is what helps them live beyond the chaos. Yet, after about a year, the chaos is gone. It's gone because the structure has settled their life into a comfortable routine. This is when the principled life begins to take root. These new people begin to live not out of right and wrong structure, but out of the principles and how they shape and affect their life with Jesus for the better. They have tested the structure and found that it works. Now they begin digging deeper, beyond right/wrong, beyond Bible prophecies and end-time events and they begin to investigate the big principles and great themes in scripture. They are building on the structure, but adding to it for their larger, biblical worldview.

After about five to ten years in, many people move into the life-integration. This is where many longtime Seventh-day Adventists are. Their kids have always been Adventist. Their life is normal around Adventists. Their friends are almost all Adventist. At this stage of life, however, many Adventists do not like the brochures or the meetings in evangelism.[47] They are no longer living in chaos. They have adopted the structure and found it works and have moved into life-integration. The brochures are no longer targeted at them. The seminar is old news, not new news. They are not in chaos, and do not see the need for the structure anymore. In fact, the materials that are targeted at people in chaos often makes the established Adventist cringe.

Recently a member came to me and said, "I have a suggestion." My staff and I have always made ourselves open to people's suggestions. So, I was all ears.

"I understand we're having another seminar in February. Can we do a brochure that doesn't have beasts on them. Can we simply have a nice picture of Jesus, maybe of the second coming?"

In truth, since I have been here at this church, we have only done one brochure with beasts on them. That was the seminar that this lady first attended which resulted in her baptism eight years ago. She has moved into the integration stage and she is no

---

[47] Sahlin, M. (2008). *Adventist Church Growth & Evangelism Research: Briefing for Presidents Council of the Pacific Union Conference* (p. 11). Westlake Village, CA: Monte Sahlin Live Presentation.

longer comfortable with the very thing that actually drew her to the meeting in the first place.

Often you will still see these long-time Adventists come to an evangelistic seminar and get rebaptized following a personal crisis of faith, health or family. They have moved back into chaos and need the structure once again, to renew their faith and trust in the Savior. This same lady, was just rebaptized last year after a seminar.

I have members who tell me they do not like the meetings. They tell me they do not like the beast brochures. My response, "That's good! They are not targeted at you. If you liked them, I would be worried that we would be unable to attract any new people!" It's called targeting. We utilize it because we are trying to reach people who are open to hearing our message.

Evangelism Intelligence is realizing who you are targeting and understanding why they would even come. There are certainly ways to reach people who live in the principled or life-integration quadrant of change, but the reason evangelism still works is because of who it is targeted to reach. The target of evangelism is those who are in chaos or crisis. The structure of evangelism is designed for it.

Money and Focus

We have already talked about the cost of evangelism. Yet, I want to say it again. You cannot do an effective evangelistic series in the 21st century on a 1950s budget. Everything costs more today. So, the church is going to have to raise more money to do what it has been called to do.

Twenty-five years ago, the conference would pay 2/3rds of every evangelistic seminar we did. If we spent $25,000 and they would give me $16,500 towards the meeting. Today, most conferences are sending $3,000-5,000 for up to one seminar per year for the local church to use.[48] That is woefully inadequate for today's budgets. My church usually spends $35,000-45,000 twice a year on evangelistic seminars. This means that most churches need to raise money if they plan to do evangelism effectively.

---

[48] This is the current Oregon Conference policy.
https://orgcministerial.netadvent.org/uploaded_assets/288955

I understand that not every church is going to do evangelism twice a year with a mailing of 80,000-120,000 homes each time. However, that does not release most churches from the need to raise money and raise enough to do the seminar adequately.

Sometimes that scares churches or pastors. "We can't meet our monthly budget and school subsidy. How could we ever raise that?" However, what I have found, is that there are certain people in each church that love evangelism and will give to it. Some pastors are scared to try to raise the money. They are scared to ask. What I say is, we cannot let the money lead the vision, the vision needs to lead the money. What's the worst that can happen? People say no?

I remember in one church where I was the associate pastor. We were making plans for an upcoming evangelistic seminar. At the finance committee, one man went off on a bit of a tirade about how it was wasted money and we should spend that money on socials instead. My senior pastor made it clear that 1) we already had a lot of money in the social committee fund, and 2) this money came from the Conference and could not be spent any other way.

One of the finance committee members spoke up and said, he would personally see to it that the social committee AND the evangelism had enough money. He was committed to evangelism and also answered the objection of the other member at the same time. He had the means to back up his statement. We went forward and after the seminar was done, the social-only-spender came and said, he was wrong, and he was glad for what happened.

Obviously, money alone does not make a successful evangelistic series. I have seen unsuccessful evangelism even with an adequate budget. Yet, I do know that you cannot reach any level of effectiveness without an adequate budget.

What I tell people is, "It's just as much work to do a series where we see three people baptized as when we see 30. I would rather spend the money and truly reap a harvest." I will say it again, a budget from the conference of $3,000-5,000 is woefully inadequate in today's climate. The church will need to come up with new ways to raise money for evangelism. The conference will need to find new ways of raising money to fund evangelism as well.

Leadership

One area of evangelism that needs a huge emphasis is that the church leadership must be behind this effort. My churches have been focused on reaching lost people. We could debate this for a long time about what the focus of the church should be. My bias is plenty obvious by now. Yet, understand that unless church leadership is behind the seminar, it's not going to work.

There was a time when the church leadership was behind me on the upcoming seminar, except for one affluent member. He was vocally opposed and was a rather loud talker in the lobby of our small church. Things finally came to a head when our guest evangelist was speaking at church, before the opening night of the seminar. This loud member confronted me in the lobby of the church. He threatened to walk up to the stage and take the mic away from the speaker. I simply looked at this man (I was in my 20s, a young, green pastor and he was in his 50s a well-to-do and respected member) and said as calmly as I could, "If you do that, before you are done, the police will come, and I'll have you arrested for trespassing." He took me seriously, because as the confrontation had built, the leaders of the church had gathered around to support me. Everyone knew what was going on in this church and what was important. In spite of this confrontation, we baptized 47 people in that seminar.

As a young green pastor, I could stand up to this man because I knew the leadership was behind me. They understood the value of growing the kingdom through evangelistic means. As an aside, the loud member who was opposed, later came back and said he agreed with me and that he respected me more for standing up to him.

Your church leadership needs to understand what I tell my churches all the time. The one spiritual gift that quits working when we get to heaven is evangelism. Once we get to the kingdom, there is no need to evangelize anymore. It is a spiritual gift. It needs to be utilized. Yet, someday it's going away. Let us use it while we can.

The Great Commission[49] was given so that we would share the gospel and bring new people in. The Great Commission was given to win, build and send people to grow the kingdom spiritually and physically. The success of any church is not its seating capacity, but its sending capacity.

Prayer

Lest anyone think evangelism is strictly about spending money and doing things right, let me set the record straight. Although I do believe that evangelism should be done correctly, without prayer as the very foundation of what we do, it will certainly fail. Evangelism Intelligence MUST include a good quantity of prayer.

We are told, "Why should the sons and daughters of God be reluctant to pray, when prayer is the key in the hand of faith to unlock heaven's storehouse, where are treasured the boundless resources of Omnipotence?"[50] If we are not willing to pray, will God unlock the community around us?

Psalm 2:8 says, "Ask of me, and I will make the nations your heritage, and the ends of the earth your possession."[51] God promises us the nations around us, we just need to ask of him. Jesus is clear about this also, "Then he said to his disciples, 'The harvest is plentiful but the workers are few. Ask the Lord of the harvest, therefore, to send out workers into his harvest field.'"[52] The emphasis on this text is two-fold. The harvest has plenty of people and we need to pray to God to get them harvested.

To emphasize that prayer is the foundation of what we must do, I want to leave you with two stories to conclude this chapter.

In Sweet Home, Oregon, we were getting ready for an evangelistic seminar. It was a dysfunctional church with a small crowd of only 40 people coming to church. We gathered two

---

[49] Matthew 28:19-20

[50] White, E. G. (1892). *Steps to Christ* (pp. 94–95). Pacific Press Publishing Association.

[51] *The Holy Bible: English Standard Version.* (2016). (Ps 2:8). Wheaton: Standard Bible Society.

[52] *The Holy Bible: New International Version.* (1984). (Mt 9:37–38). Grand Rapids, MI: Zondervan.

weeks before the seminar began. We gathered to confess our sin, to plead with God, and to ask for success. I was a new minister and knew almost nothing about doing evangelism properly. We gathered and prayed that Sabbath morning after church. We prayed again on Wednesday night. We prayed the next Sabbath and Wednesday again. About half of our congregation gathered at each of these prayer sessions. Many of the church had been praying about this for several months leading up to this time.

Our little church, although only 40 in attendance, could seat 250 people. We did not know what to expect, but our evangelist had taught us a lot about advertising, spending the right amount of money. We did it by the book. Opening night, a miracle happened. More than 350 people came and we had to set up every chair we could find. We set them up in the aisles, in the lobby, and nearly on the platform. We owned 100 chairs. We were in shock. The evangelist was in shock. In the end, we baptized 43 people and doubled the size of our congregation!

In the wake of doubling the size of my church in a matter of a few weeks, I was asked all kinds of things, quoted in emails, and people began to visit to see what we were up against. The most famous quote by me during that time was, "Evangelism isn't dead, but I am!" Yet, it was my wife who would remind me what really happened when she would regularly ask me, "Isn't it great to be part of something so big, that wasn't designed or orchestrated by you?" Yes, we worked hard to get all the details right.. However, we all knew – *the church members, the evangelist, and my family* – this was a result of prayer. The Holy Spirit had moved, and we simply rode the wave while He pushed it.

Another time, after many years in ministry and about 35 or 40 evangelistic series under our belt, we prepared for an upcoming seminar, this one in Vancouver, Washington. We prepared the teams of volunteers, arranged for refreshments, prepared the lobby decorations, made sure the backdrop was standing correct and worked our systems properly. We were still doing everything by the book.

However, we never got the church out to pray. We got busy and forgot. We had a prominent evangelist coming and we expected with our knowledge and his experience, we would be fine by the numbers. In fact, this was the exact same evangelist who years before when we had worked together, we had seen the miracle in Sweet Home, Oregon. However, tragedy struck before the seminar even began. Only half of the brochures were delivered before the seminar began. Half of those, 25%, were delivered the day of the seminar, which was essentially too late. About 25% of the brochures got delivered two and a half weeks into the seminar and about 25% never got delivered at all. The seminar was a complete flop as to reaching people. There were no new people who joined our church as a result.

In the end, we all knew – *the church members, the evangelist, and my family* – this was a result of not praying. We had taken on a job and we had left out the Holy Spirit. It was a sad day when we swallowed hard and confessed our sin of relying upon ourselves.

Nothing moves in the kingdom of God without prayer. E.M. Bounds says prayer is not preparation for the battle. It is not equipping us for a greater work. Rather, "Prayer is the battle."[53] In this instance we found out that forgetting to pray for God's power, for His Spirit to bind up the community did not happen, and we lost the battle. When Ellen White says, "…prayer is the key in the hand of faith to unlock heaven's storehouse…"[54] she is forewarning us that unless we pray, the lock stays locked.

Today, before we launch any evangelistic initiative, we begin with a season of prayer. We have learned the hard way that Evangelism Intelligence is learning to rely more upon the Holy Spirit than upon our systems and procedures and fundraising. The church must understand this key part. Yes, we need to understand why evangelism works, but in the end, the real equation shows that evangelism works because it is Holy Spirit empowered. No matter your attitude about evangelism, if your initiative is being led by prayer, the church will see evangelism success. We have done simple prayer meetings, prayer times before and after church, anointing services, and 40 days of prayer time.

---

[53] E.M.Bounds – http://utmost.org/the-key-of-the-greater-work/
[54] White, E. G. (1892). *Steps to Christ* (p. 94). Pacific Press Publishing Association.

6

Do It By The Book

 In the summers during college, I did door-to-door sales. I was successful enough at it to pay my way through college and become a leader of other students. As a leader, we trained other students how to do things properly, gave them courage to begin and sent them out. The training was a very intense two-week training in the classroom and on the streets. My primary task through the summer, as a leader, was to work with the various students throughout the week, encourage them, train more, and help them stay motivated. I usually had ten to fifteen students I worked with all summer. Each day I would be in a different place. I would be in Salem, Oregon working with a student one day, the next in Portland, and the next in Castle Rock, Washington. Each day I would seek to watch them, encourage them, and help them improve what they were doing.

 Invariably, I would show up to help someone early in the summer when they were not selling well. The students were excited to have help and wanted me to sell some books for them, or they were going to leave the summer broke! They wanted me to begin selling immediately as we began the day. Rather than jump right in doing the selling myself, I would let the student know on the first few doors that I would watch how they were trying to sell books. If I went first, they would copy me and I would not see what they were doing or what was going wrong.

After watching the student for a while, I would drive to a park and we would get out and take a break. Usually I asked something like this: "Why aren't you doing the canvass we taught you?"[55] The student's inevitable answer was, "It just wasn't me. The canvass felt stiff and I didn't like it. So, I made up my own."

I would lean closer and tell them as kindly as I could, ***"THAT'S WHY YOU AREN'T SELLING ANYTHING!"*** The rest of the day would be spent trying to teach them that until they were successful at the proven success method – whether they liked it or not – they would never understand the sales process enough to experiment on their own. Some of the students got it. Unfortunately, some of them never did. In other words, only those who "get it" know enough to experiment.

It is the same with evangelism. I know too many pastors who do not "get it." These pastors continue to say, "I don't like the way it's done, so I'm going to come up with my own method." Unfortunately, most of these pastors never get it and they continue to take their church through unsuccessful evangelism attempts until they finally quit trying, because they eventually say, "Evangelism doesn't work anymore." They are wrong.

Recently a pastor friend called me and asked if I would help him prepare for doing an evangelistic series. I am always pleased to coach someone to get better at reaching lost people, so of course I told him I would. My pastor friend then told me to go to his church's website, because he had been preaching the evangelistic messages on Sabbath morning in preparation for a possible upcoming seminar. He said he loved doing it and he thought they were great sermons.

My friend is a great pastor. He is loved by his congregation and he does preach great sermons. However, as I listened to his sermons, I realized that these were great sermons for the already convinced to get reacquainted with their beliefs, but they were not evangelistic messages. It was painfully obvious they were not going to work. Hopefully, the rest of this chapter will tell you why. This is the nuts and bolts of evangelism intelligence that dives into the science of doing evangelism correctly.

To those who will listen, I tell them, "Find a successful evangelistic program and preach it by the book." In other words:

---

[55] What I meant was the sales process – door approach, introduction of the books, and closing the sale.

1. Preach the proven evangelistic sermons with very little changes except maybe the illustrations *(but be careful even with those)*
2. Learn the process of why evangelistic sermons are given in a certain order
3. Learn how to make a successful call
4. Learn how to preach not for information, but for decisions
5. Add your own testimony to the mix and share other's testimonies too.

After people are successful following these basic rules of evangelism, then they can begin to experiment and remain successful.[56] Yet someone will eventually tell me, "I don't like those sermons, they aren't me. They are stiff and I don't like them." I tell those people, "So what if it isn't you? When have you ever learned something new that you were immediately comfortable doing?" It's a rare person that can just make new things happen without going through a learning curve.

Let us walk through those five steps individually for a few minutes.

Preach Proven Sermons

First, find a series of evangelistic sermons from Mark Finley, Russell Burrill, or from an established evangelist who will share his/her material, and begin learning it.[57] If possible, attend a

---

[56] I suggest anywhere from 2-5 successful series before experimenting. It all depends on whether you succeed and on the speaker's experience with evangelism in general. Success is defined in this instance as the evangelism was effective at getting decisions.

[57] You can find those series from ASI, It Is Written, in books, or often sitting on a shelf in the local Conference office. If you are looking for some sermons, you can download for free the latest sermons from It Is Written at http://seriesbuilder.com/. That's the main site for them, you can order their material for a fee, or just click on the link for free downloads. They are available in PDF, Keynote, or PowerPoint. Or you can download from the ASI site - https://asiministries.org/newbeginnings/ in a variety of languages. Also, another spot is: www.sharehim.org

seminar where these sermons are being used and take copious notes about how the speaker times things, how he pauses, what speed he speaks at, the emphasis he draws out, etc. Sure, take the illustrations out that tell about preaching in Russia to thousands of people, and add your own. However, resist the urge to completely rewrite the messages. Do not change what has worked in evangelism to something that has not worked nor even been tried before.

I asked one person why he had significantly changed a crucial evangelistic message. His response, "My wife didn't like that one." I was thinking, "You asked me to coach you because you didn't know how to do evangelism. Why would you listen to your wife when she knows even less about how evangelism works than you?" Shaking my head…. I will say it again and again; Evangelism Intelligence means doing it by the book until you figure out **WHY** and **HOW** it works.

Next, learn how to preach well with a manuscript. Many people do not like preaching from a manuscript, but it affords you some benefits: 1) you never wonder about what is coming next, 2) someone else can follow along and change slides for you if necessary, 3) if nerves are a problem and you lose your place, it's very easy to find your place and start again.

However, preaching from a manuscript is not just reading. It's learning to use your voice inflection, speed of delivery and even eye contact to make it appear as if it's not just reading. Do not worry too much about reading anyway, most people in evangelism are watching the slides more than the speaker anyway.

Evangelism is a fine balance between information, decisions and Holy Spirit conviction. Keep the sermon together and if need be, preach from the manuscript that was put together.

I am not a manuscript preacher. In fact, on a regular Sabbath morning, I do not even preach with notes. I preach that way at church because my job on Sabbath mornings is to connect with people, not my manuscript. Evangelism is not about connecting (although that doesn't hurt), it's primarily about decisions. When I do evangelism, I preach with a healthy supply of notes and often a manuscript.

While church planting for 11 years, I brought in outside evangelists almost every time. When I moved to Vancouver, Washington, I was rusty in doing evangelism. So, I took my own advice and I did two series by the book until I saw some success again. I preached some old sermons. These sermons were not the greatest evangelistic sermons ever written. However, I knew they worked for others and I had used them in the past. The first series, I had my daughter run the slides, so I could focus on the preaching. She simply followed the manuscript with me as I preached. We baptized 15 people. The second series I ran my own slides but made very few changes, just had a new system of using my iPhone® in hand for notes and advancing the slides. It was easy. After that, I put together a brand-new series and still had 15 more baptisms.

In other words, I take my own advice when it comes to doing evangelism by the book.

Learn the Order of the Messages

There is a rhyme and reason as to why we preach certain things and in what order we preach them. If you understand this grid – you will see two things:

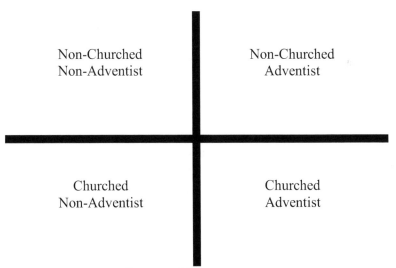

Figure 6-1: Barrier Crossing Matrix

First, in Figure 6-1 above, to cross from the top half to the bottom half is a spiritual barrier. This is where people discover who Jesus is and take the time to accept Him. It's a barrier, but it's a spiritual one. Will they put Jesus Christ first and foremost in their lives?

Second, to cross from left to right, you cross a theological barrier. To move from Non-Adventist to Adventist, you must deal with a different day of worship, a different belief about death, about the second coming, and many other things. This is a theological barrier

So, to move from Unchurched, non-Adventist to Churched Adventist, you must cross both barriers – a spiritual one and a theological barrier. It's not easy, and because of that, there is a certain order to the messages we present.

If you talk with successful evangelists, they will tell you that they seek to present only one new, major topic a week. They may use a different order, but the point is they follow this concept. The first week they present the second coming of Christ. This is the key message in crossing the theological barrier in the first 4-5 nights. But it's not a major issue in the whole skew of things.

The second coming is a theological barrier and it will cause few people to leave. It's a new way of understanding, but it does not change anyone's life. So, they present it first.

Next comes the state of death. This is a tougher one to get over, because no one wants to imagine their Aunt Mary in the grave. They would much rather have their father or mother in heaven, then in a grave. Heaven means happiness, grave means rotting and death. They show up to the meeting with Uncle Henry in heaven, and they leave with him in the grave? Emotions run high because they want their friend or loved one in heaven. In almost 30 years of ministry, I have only done one funeral where the family does not believe that individual was already in heaven. This family thought he was already burning in Hell. (See Chapter 2 for that whole story.)

The theological and emotional barrier of death is hard for people, and it will scare some away, but not most. It's a change of status and it's hard, so we do not present it the first week. We wait till we have proven our trustworthiness with scripture. We wait until they are captivated enough to keep coming.

Next is the Sabbath. It's not only a theological barrier to cross, it's also emotional because it changes what the whole world teaches. However, it also crosses a lifestyle barrier. The Sabbath requires a change that will make people different from anyone they know.

It takes time to process some of these barrier crossings. So, that is also why we preach some of the non-decision messages like the Millennium, heaven, or other so-called soft-topics. Two basic reasons to preach those soft messages: 1) it's a chance to reiterate some of the previous message ideas and 2) It allows time to process the harder decisions. In other words, there is one main point to make per week. It also allows them time to process and filter the new information. The rest of it is designed to support that one big decision.

Learn to Make Calls

One of the key things that happen at evangelism is DECISIONS. People tend to make decisions at events, they maintain those decisions in a small group of close friends. So, even though an evangelistic sermon is full of information, the key to the sermon is not the information, but the actual call for a decision.

Once, my two associates and I shared the speaking at an evangelistic series. Since neither of them had ever done any evangelism before, we agreed to do it by the book. To set the example, I took the hard messages and I preached them as they were written. Exactly. But because of the nature of the series, we had to adjust how the calls were made.

One of my associates struggled with preaching by the book. He adapted the messages and changed the points. I was not okay with that, yet, I was handling the really crucial messages and there was room to breathe a little in these sermons. However, I gave him the opportunity to make one of the calls. I figured it would be good for him. We went over it in staff meeting, step-by-step. We had changed the pre-printed card to adjust for something else going on.

He preached a good message, albeit he did not follow the notes at all. But when it came time for the call, he followed the pre-printed notes as they were written in his manuscript. Exactly. This was the only thing he followed in the manuscript, yet this was the one thing we had specifically changed. This was what we had gone over, and he missed what the card said that the people had in their hands. The people were lost. It was a blown opportunity for a successful call.

The call is the one area you want to be sure and memorize. It's the one thing where the words are crucial. This is no time to stumble. It is a time to be direct, look people in the eye and not be afraid to put your audience on the spot. It must be bathed in prayer as you seek to move people towards a decision.

Too many pastors try to do evangelism and fail. It's been said that pastors will get less decisions than an evangelist. I have found that to be basically true. It's often because of this one area – calls. Pastor's do not like putting people on the spot. They do not like pushing for a decision, so they back off. Pastors often try to take the heat off someone, but it could be the Holy Spirit who is bringing that heat to them. We cannot apologize for asking people to decide. We must step in with both feet and learn how to give a call in a way that really asks for a decision. No mumbling or stumbling.

Another aspect of calls comes from an old sales technique. Little decisions lead to big decisions. All along the way, we get people to nod their heads, shake their heads and agree with us. We get them making small raised hands decisions on messages that are not crucial, simply because we know that will help them to make make more important decisions later. That is what we are talking about in this next section.

Preach for Decisions

Everything you preach should be leading people to make that decision. Little decisions lead to the bigger ones. It is not just the call we make on a given night, the decision process is a night-by-night affair. It is also moment-by-moment as you preach. So, you cannot just stop after speaking about the information, you must speak as if the information is life-changing because…well…it is!

The information is faith-changing. However, the sermon must go beyond the basic preaching of information. The sermon must include little decisions that lead to the bigger decision. In other words, the climax of the night is not when Nebuchadnezzar comes to grips with his dream and that Daniel knows some amazing stuff. No, the crux of what is said during the sermon is building towards the call to action in the last few minutes of the message.

This is the stuff you need to memorize. Every message must have a call. Here is a list of some of the types of calls I utilize:

1. Simply saying something like, "I want you to think about this as you go home tonight…."
2. A Raised Hand – "How many of you think this is true?"
3. Stand for prayer if you agree
4. Kneel for prayer if you want to make this decision
5. Card Call – fill out a decision card
6. Card and come forward
7. Come Forward
8. Personal visits and calls in the home or the church office

Each night, as I am preaching, I say things like, "Am I making sense?" or "You agree with that, don't you?" Those are about getting buy-in. Things like a nodded head, clapping, "amen" are all part of getting little decisions to help people make bigger decisions.

Add a Testimony

There is almost nothing as powerful as a personal testimony. I have a friend who is of Iraqi descent and was beaten when he made the decision to keep the Sabbath. I know people who have lost their jobs for the Sabbath and have never looked back and wondered if they should not have made that decision. Someone who lost their five children in a brutal murder found amazing hope in the state of the dead.

Of course, the most powerful testimony you can share is your own. You do not have to manufacture anything from your story to fit each sermon. Yet, if it fits, it will add credibility to what you are saying. Your testimony cannot be argued with. It is your story. It also adds a level of emotion to the message, moving it away from facts alone.

For me, I have several aspects of my own testimony that I share. I talk about keeping the Sabbath and how that affected my first career desire of playing professional baseball. I talk about my decision to submit to Christ on the night of the message of salvation. I tell a story about visiting my grandparents when I talk about the second coming. Each are a part of my story.

Adding a personal story allows people to connect with you and lets them know that you are sincere in what you are preaching. If you do not think you have a personal story (you do!), share someone else's story.

My point in this chapter is to give you some handles to do evangelism by the book. If you find that you are not successful at evangelism, start by doing it by the book. Once you reach a level of success, then begin to experiment. Let me say one last thing about experiments.

One time I did an evangelistic seminar that we had not tried before. We had three speakers (experiment one), it went on weekends only (experiment two), the time frame was a bit of an experiment (experiment 3), and my two associates had never done any speaking for evangelism before (experiment 4). We had never preached these sermons before (experiment 5). In the end, it was one of our worst series for results I have ever had. The conclusion we came to was this: we had too many experiments at once. We couldn't measure what actually happened. There were too many experiments to see what was going wrong. Every individual aspect of the seminar was an experiment for us. We did not play it by the book enough. In the end, the number of experiments meant we had no way to measure what worked and what did not.

So, for people who want to experiment, I recommend that they try one experiment per seminar. If they want to push for more, I encourage them try one major and one minor experiment. Too many experiments create too many variables to measure what went right and what went wrong. If we are going to experiment, we should also come up with some measurables so we know whether we should try that experiment again or not. Too often, people see their experiment did not work, throw it out and never try again. Yet, if the experiment is carefully monitored and measured, you know how to try it again. Then, you haven't wasted your time with an experiment.

7

Creating A Culture of Evangelism in Your Church

One day, in Colorado, an elderly couple, Lee and Patti, showed up at our church. Their first Sabbath they informed us they were moving their membership from a very traditional church with an average age of 71 to ours. We were a contemporary church plant with an average age of 30. "Why do you want to transfer your membership?" I queried. It wasn't clear whether they would fit our target, our age, or our style. Would they like what they saw? Later, I found out my fears were unfounded. What they said, saddened me.

Lee and Patti explained, "Last week, we had a tremendous opportunity to take our neighbor to church. She had always said no, this time she said 'Yes!' As you can imagine, we were very excited about bringing her to church." They had been talking to her for quite some time about God, church, and the cross of Christ. They had invited her to church many times, but she had always refused. However, the week before I met them, she decided to go with them to church. When Lee and Patti picked her up for church, they were excited, friendly and were ready for a great day. Their friend was nervous but looking forward to what was in store for the day.

Lee continued, "As we walked from the parking lot to the front steps, we were met by the so-called greeter. She simply looked down the steps at us and said directly to our neighbor, "We don't come to church dressed like that. Then she never said,

'Welcome' 'Hello' 'Glad you are here.' Rather, she just turned around and walked back into the building leaving us standing there flat-footed and slack-jawed. Our friend turned several shades of red and we weren't sure whether it was anger or embarrassment."

It's sad that this ill-informed greeter saw someone coming who was obviously a guest and felt the need to correct her on the first moment she stepped onto the church property. With their neighbor in shock, and now refusing to go in, Lee and Patti took her home. They then told me, "We aren't going back. That church is not ready for new people. We want to come here, because you have a church that is ready for new people." It's true. We had created a church with a culture for outreach and evangelism.

Is Church for Insiders, or Outsiders?

Too often, the church is only concerned about what happens inside the church and does not realize that people outside the church matter and we should be attracting them. Many times, new people want in, but we have closed the doors and do not even realize they are trying to get in. We cannot even imagine a new person coming in. We are more concerned about paying the bills, what's going on at the local church school, and all that happens inside the church than about those that live a stone's throw away from our churches.

One of the ways that we do that is in our insider language. Every group has insider language. Some may be familiar with the military and their acronyms, families and their inside jokes and stories, company culture, etc. We all do it. Yet, the church is the one organization that should be reaching beyond the insider language because we are not trying to keep people out, we want more people with us. However, we stick to our insider jargon all the time.

When I first attended church as a 12-year-old boy. I remember overhearing an elderly lady say something to another elderly lady what sounded like, "Are you coming with us, you dork?" My jaw must have dropped to my knees because later when my mom asked me about it she said, "I think what she said was, "Are you coming with us to Dorcas?" She went on to explain to me what Dorcas was.

Here are some more examples of our insider language. Try to picture them as what others hear when they hear the term for the first time. These are actual things people have said to me and what they thought they heard.

- Dork Us!
- Gee See
- Please turn in your ties and offerings
- Allan B. White
- New Tina
- Loam and Linda
- Pot Luck
- Cradle Roll
- Path Finders
- Investment

When you stop and think about some of those terms from the perspective of someone who has never heard them in our church setting, it must make you stop and wonder! Why would we roll cradles? Why do I want a new Tina, what's wrong with the old Tina? Although I have never seen anyone remove their tie and put in the offering plate, it does make for an interesting picture. I actually had a lady come up to me one day, after she had attended our church for nearly two years. She said to me, "Roger, who is Allen B. White? I keep hearing his name in Sabbath School classes...." After two years she was still mishearing it!

Insider language. How do you fix it? Well, actually you cannot fully fix it. We are going to use some of those terms periodically. That's fairly normal. However, what I seek to train my church to do is to go ahead and say what you want to say, but explain yourself to the new person. If we are constantly aware that there may be new people in our midst we might stop and wonder some time.

So, recently at our first service, a lady announced something about the "Gee See." I challenged her in the back room before the second service to be aware of the guests or new members and say something like, "Recently I was attending a meeting at the General Conference. That is the world headquarters of the Seventh-day Adventist Church in the Washington DC area." She agreed that would be good and she did it perfectly at our second service. All she had to do was simply explain herself.

There is nothing wrong with people saying things newcomers do not understand, if we explain ourselves.

I never say things like, "Our favorite author…" or "Sister White says…." Why? Because the guests do not get it. So, I say things like, "In a book on the life of Christ, called the Desire of Ages, it says this…." The new people are not scared away; the members understand what I am doing, and we are learning to be guest friendly. It's one step in creating a culture of evangelism.

The next step to making evangelism part of the church's culture is directed in the chart below. Start at the bottom, the foundation, and work yourself up towards the top. Some churches take about 18 months to get through this cycle. Others do it twice a year or more.

Figure 7-1: Culture of Evangelism Pyramid

Understanding this chart is key to understanding how to create a culture of evangelism in any church. Step by step, we build from the foundation of friendship and work ourselves up to the top. Allow me to explain.

Friendship

Start by building the foundation of a spirit of friendship in your church. Help the members 1) learn to like themselves, but 2) more importantly, learn to make friends with people outside the church. I tell people the goal of this is *redemptive* friendships. In other words, the goal is to ultimately lead the people to Christ. You may not be the person to do it, but build an honest friendship with people who are outside the holy huddle and welcome them into your lives. Share, learn, listen, encourage, and ultimately — we hope — they will ask about your religion or your help with a spiritual problem in their lives.

The goal is true, honest friendships. We are not trying to build a friendship with an agenda. We are not trying to make people into a project. No, we are simply rubbing shoulders with people on a day-to-day basis hoping to share the gospel with them when they are ready.

Bob heard me talking about redemptive friendships, only he missed the redemptive part. So, he and his wife, both relatively new members themselves, wanted to follow through on making friends. They loved making friends. They loved the church. If making friends could grow the church, then they were in.

The next week they were on cloud nine! Their excitement knew no bounds. They told me all about how they had met Stacy and Roland and had taken them drinking and dancing to build a friendship with them. It did not take me longer than 2.5 nanoseconds to realize they had missed the redemptive side of this equation. I quickly applauded them for trying, so I would not discourage their enthusiasm, but spent some time discipling them on the idea of what the redemptive side of friendship means and, in this case, what it does not mean.

- Do not follow them into their sin
- Invite them to church
- Invite them to come up, don't go down to their level
- Open up spiritual conversations

- When troubles come, show them Jesus to whom you turn
- Do not worry about doctrinal things right now
- Make a friend, and include Jesus with you
- Be a support and help to them
- Take them to dinner, not drinking.
- Go to the park with both sets of kids
- Spend time in hobbies
- Invite their family to spend time with your family
- Share your tools
- Help them in their yard/garden
- Volunteer to pick up something for them at the store
- Much more could be thought of....

Building a culture of redemptive friendships is important to the overall culture of evangelism. After being in the church for 7 years, the average church member has no friends outside the church. So, reaching the lost never crosses their minds. Having people who are friends that do not go to church changes one's perspective about what the church is about.

If your church can become a church of inviters, it will make a huge impact on the growth of the church and the kingdom.

Pastors must lead the charge in this. I remember two very specific things in the same church.

One friend of mine told me "Thanks Rog, for leading the charge on redemptive friendships. You really do talk about this a lot. But you are the first pastor I've met that also does it." I was thankful that God had pushed me this direction. My friend was also catching the vision.

On another occasion, a lady came to me after I had preached again on redemptive friendships. She said, "You talk about this probably more than anything I've heard you talk about. But 'we' don't know how to make friends. You need to teach us how to do that."

My first thought was, "Oh come on! You don't know how to make friends?!?! COME ON!" Fortunately, I did not respond that way. As I thought about it, talked it over with people, I realized that many – too many – people do not know the first thing about making friends. They need that understanding.

We used to build houses with porches on them. We used to walk in our neighborhoods. As we walked around, we would stop and talk to our neighbors who were sitting on their porches. Not today. Today the front porch is barely big enough for two people to stand out of the rain while they unlock their doors. The houses are bigger and people would rather sit in front of their 65" TV rather than sit and talk with their neighbors. People are lonely, and they do not even know the name of their next-door neighbor.

One day my wife went strawberry picking. We were newly married and lived in an apartment complex. Our door was in the same section of six doors. Two doors on the basement floor, two in the middle and two on top. My wife decided to share some strawberries with our neighbors. We had only waved to them up to this time.

She knocked on one door and the lady was surprised to see her. Gail explained why she was there and they lady almost started crying. She said, "I've lived here for two years and have been so lonely that I'm moving next week. I don't know anyone." After chatting for a few moments, Gail went to the next door.

"I've lived here for about a year and am going to move. I don't know anyone here." Gail was amazed. Even more amazing it happened at the next door too.

"I've lived here for 15 years and don't know anyone," The lady right above us complained. In 5 doors, she heard the same basic story 3 times. To be fair, the other two apartments, no one was home.

People all around us are lonely. As leaders we must teach our people to reach out in kindness. Friendships will happen. Pastors need to start by teaching their members how to make redemptive friendships and how to be an inviter. My goal in redemptive friendships is that the members are constantly working on building them. We should talk about this weekly from the front of the church. We should find people who can share testimonies about this.

When Gail and I bought our first house, it was 40 years old and we were the second owners. People would stop and say, "You bought the Olson's House! Mr. Olson used to sit in a chair by those windows and smoke his cigarettes, drink his coffee and he would always wave to us." We heard that from so many neighbors, that we decided that even though we were not coffee drinkers or smokers, we could continue the household tradition of waving as people drove or walked by.

We've been waving to people ever since. This has opened up all kinds of friendships while we go for walks. It's opened up all kinds of conversations that we might not otherwise have.

One time while we walked, we saw a sign for a garage sale, and we walked over to see it. The lady of the house said to us, "Oh! You are the walkers!" "I thought, "No, we are the Walter's" She continued, "you guys are always so happy, and you always wave as I drive by."

Friendship can begin in as simple a way as waving to neighbors. Have a neighborhood barbecue, invite a neighbor to go on a hike with you, talk about how their lawn looks, take a loaf of bread next door, bake some Christmas cookies and deliver to your neighborhood, invite someone to go to dinner. You will be amazed at how a small gesture will open up more conversation and soon, friendship happens. Just be friendly.

Kindness

The next layer of the pyramid is Kindness Evangelism, also called Servant Evangelism. It is the next step in the culture of evangelism process. Kindness Evangelism involves baking bread for friends and neighbors, it might be picking up trash in the park, cleaning someone's home, or washing windshields in the Walmart parking lot – just to show God's love in a practical way. It is a natural outgrowth of the redemptive friendship layer.

Kindness Evangelism projects are low-level entry points. Anyone can do them. They are not confrontive. They are not hard to do. They are simply adding to the culture of service in the community. They are done outside the walls of the church with a small group of people to reach into their community with random acts of kindness.

Some of the things we have done for Kindness Evangelism are these:

- We have gone into Walmart with squirt bottles, rags and squeegees and began washing windshields in the parking lot. We left a little card under the windshield wiper that said, "While you were gone, we washed your windshield, just to show you God's love in a practical way." On the back of the card was church information and a map.

- We have passed out 9-volt batteries door-to-door saying, "We just wanted to remind you to change your smoke alarm batteries. We included a similar card as above.
- We have gone out on Saturday afternoons to the county fair or to the soccer fields and handed out water bottles, "Just to show you God's love in a practical way."
- We went to the Hospital and handed flowers to the nurses, attendants and patients, just to show God's love....
- Some have cleaned toilets
- Some have washed business windows
- Others handed out hot chocolate in the cold wintry park
- Still others have regular community picnics, where they barbecued what people would eat
- Others have mowed grass, cleaned houses, did a community pick up.[58]

The idea behind this is to get people in your church thinking beyond themselves. It can be done with as few as one or two people and as many as 25 at a time. These are small activities. Kids get involved, elderly can do it, and it's fun. By doing these kinds of activities in the community, you create a sense of community in the church and begin breaking down the barriers to reaching people.

Once, we took a group of about 15 kids and adults and stood in front of the county fair with ice-cold water bottles. On each of the bottles was a note that said, "We just wanted to refresh you with God's love in a practical way, no strings attached."

The crowd was moving quickly and too many people to stand and talk to, but one lady stopped and came up to me. While my kids kept handing water bottles, she said, "What church

---

[58] Visit www.servantevangelism.com, or www.kindnessresources.com for many more ideas

sponsors this?" When I told her the name of the church she said, "Oh, I've heard of them." Yay! That is a win. People began to associate us with doing acts of kindness, serving the community.

Another time, we went to local hospital with 3-4 teams of about 5 people and handed out carnations to the nurses and attendants. Attached to the carnation was a note that said, "We just wanted to say thanks for all you do in our community, in a practical way." The nurses were in shock. More importantly, my kids had a blast sharing the love of Jesus in a practical way. We all went home laughing, telling stories and sharing what others said to us.

My goal is that we would do these 2-3 times a quarter or do them monthly. However, small groups could do them without the pastoral staff getting involved and putting them on the church calendar. If a small group took to doing these, and if 5, or 10 small groups were each doing these every quarter…the impact could be very big.

Bridge

After you have built redemptive friendships, after you have served in the community, people are aware of your church and the people who attend it. Now it's time to build a bridge to the church.

This step is important. So often we only invite people to come when we are doing some major evangelistic outreach. Building a bridge from the knowledge of the church to actually attending something is vital to helping people hear the message of the cross and accept it. People make little decisions that lead to larger ones. That's what the bridge is, another small decision leading to the larger decisions.

Bridge events are simply non-religious events at the church that bring people through the doors in a non-threatening environment. Traditionally, we have done cooking schools and stop smoking clinics. We can still do those. However, others have tried financial classes, health clinics, family/parenting classes, computer tech classes, after-school latch key programs, babysitting for a parent's night out, movie night at the church and many more ideas. Other ideas might include grief recovery seminar, divorce recovery class, AA meetings, or letting a community gathering hold their monthly meetings at the church.

Most bridge events are about getting people to the church for a safe, non-threatening event. The key here is to break the ice about someone coming through the doors of the church, so they feel good about "those people" and they might be willing to come in again.

Once, we did a health fair at our church. We were on a major thoroughfare that went right into downtown Portland. Thousands of people drove by our church every day. The attendance was awesome! We set up booths in our gym. We did cholesterol screenings, scoliosis checks, sign-ups for a vegetarian cooking school, blood pressure checks, and even had a couple of doctors there who would answer individual questions and do basic physical checks. We had several hundred-people come through.

Another time we did a medical clinic with a mission group called AMEN (Adventist Medical Evangelism Network)[59] for an area-wide "Impact Your Health" weekend. There we expect to see upwards of 500 people walk through the doors of the church. Quarterly, we do another event called God's Closet, where people pay $1 to get two grocery bags and then they fill them with clothing for their kids. It's a huge undertaking, but we get 300-500 people through the doors of our church every quarter.

When you actually bridge people to the church, they begin to look with favor on many of the things you do. They like you, they are open to coming again, because in serving them, you've broken down barriers to their coming again.

The goal here is to do one or two of these bridge events, a month or two before the next reaping seminar, which is our next step in the pyramid.

Reap

Reaping, or evangelistic seminars, is what most of the rest of the book is about. I will not spend much time here, because the rest of the book talks more in depth about this. Suffice it to say that if you have laid the ground work solidly through the other steps – Friendship, Kindness, Bridge Events – when it comes time

---

[59] see www.amensda.org

for an evangelistic reaping event, your church will be ready, and you will have created a culture of evangelism. Your members will be expectant, the community will have a raised consciousness, and the Holy Spirit will be free to work to a higher level. The previous chapters talk about how to do this part of the pyramid.

Keep

Part of the process of building this culture is to not just win people, but also to keep people. I have often heard people say, "Evangelism doesn't work. We baptized some people and a year later they weren't there."[60] Generally speaking, this isn't at all true, as was expressed in an earlier chapter. I like what a friend of mine said one day in response to this. "Evangelism worked, the church didn't."[61]

What he is expressing is what is found in this chart:

---

[60] See Chapter 3 and Myth #3

[61] Chuck Burkeen, Oregon Conference Members in Ministry/Evangelism Director

Life Continuum

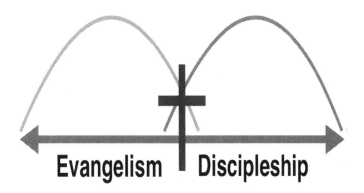

Figure 7-2 Life Continuum Chart[62]

    Everything left of the cross is evangelism. Everything right of the cross is discipleship. The focus of this book has been about things that are left of the cross. However, we cannot completely ignore what happens right of the cross. If we bring people in and lose them, what have we really done?

    Discipleship is the key. In the Great Commission, Jesus directed us, *"Therefore go and make disciples of all nations, baptizing them in the name of the Father and of the Son and of the Holy Spirit,"*[63] We do four main things to make sure the people stay and are discipled. This is not our complete discipleship program. Discipleship is not evangelism follow-up, but evangelism follow-up is part of the discipleship process.

---

[62] This is an adaptation of the Engel Scale, see:
https://en.wikipedia.org/wiki/Engel_Scale
[63] *The Holy Bible: New International Version.* (1984). (Mt 28:19–20). Grand Rapids, MI: Zondervan.

Four Ideas for Follow-up:

The first thing we do in keeping our new members is we begin a **Bible Marking class**. This is a chain reference system through much of the same material we went through in the evangelistic seminar.

We do not cover all the same material and we do not cover it from a prophecy standpoint. One of my associates or I simply share a bible verse and talk about it and the people mark their Bibles. We start with something significant, we do not follow the same order as the evangelistic process, because 95% of these people have already heard the material. Now, we are covering information to reinforce learning rather than introducing information.

In the Bible marking class we are teaching people to use their Bibles, how to mark their Bible for giving future Bible studies to others, and they are getting to know other people in the class, making friends.

We also tell them if they come to the Bible Marking Class 7 times (it is usually 12-14 weeks long), we will give them a copy of Mark Finley's book, "Studying Together."

The second thing we do is start **small group Bible studies**. Most of the new people are not prepared for how to fill their time. They have been coming 4-5 nights a week for 3-5 weeks and now want to keep studying.

A small group does several things as people get involved in them. 1) we study much of the same material in a 15-minute DVD prophecy study,[64] 2) we interact with the material in a small group study, 3) we eat together and there is a creation of social atmosphere that goes very deep in helping people integrate into the life of the church while also discipling them.

The average person needs seven close friends within the first year of joining a church or they will not stay. The creation of small groups after every evangelistic series helps people find and make those friends. Most of the time, I do not try to integrate these new people into groups that are already established. I find it's best to have a good leader and maybe one other person who is an established member and the rest are new people. Many of these

---

[64] We primarily use the *New Beginnings Small Group* materials from *It Is Written.*

groups are still meeting years later and are part of the 40 or so groups (we call them Community Groups) we have at church.

The third thing we do after our seminars is to **preach a series of messages** on Sabbath mornings that support people's decision to follow Jesus. I do not preach about the particular Bible topics they have already studied, but I usually mention their decision. I talk about how to keep decisions, how to grow, how to maintain their spiritual health and teach them how to have personal devotions.

This is a time to reinforce the gospel message they have just heard. It's also a time to strengthen their resolve to make a life-change. The messages are designed to back that up. I steer away from more controversial topics during this season of church-life and I make room for people to feel good about their decision. I make sure and use plenty of Bible verses, because the people are used to using their Bibles in the seminar.

The fourth thing we do is get **a team of mentors** who will visit these new people regularly. They usually have a book to give to them each time they visit, they take them out to eat, invite them over for Sabbath lunch, and help them understand Adventist lingo, culture and spiritual life.

One man likes to take the people he is mentoring to the Conference Office and the local Adventist Book Center. He introduces them to how the structure of the church works, where tithe dollars go, and where the new people can come to feed themselves spiritually with good books, magazines, etc.

Creating a culture of evangelism takes time. You cannot run through the cycle of Friendship, Kindness, Bridge, Reap and Keep in three months and have created a culture. Some churches will adapt to this culture very quickly. Others will not. In my current church, we followed this basic pattern and began doing two evangelistic series a year and it still took two years to begin to set that culture in place.

It's very common in my church now, for people to come up and say, "Pastor, who's doing our fall evangelistic series?" People have come to expect the culture of this church is evangelism.

One lady sent me this story. She was at the library trying to print something and was having problems. She turned to a gentleman standing there and asked if he knew how to make it work. He could not get it to print either. My member went and got one of the librarians and told her she wanted to have three copies printed. The man turned and said, could I have a copy too?

You see, while she went to get the librarian, he read the poem on the screen. He then asked my member, "What church do you attend?"

"I attend the Adventist Community Church over on St. Johns Rd." she said.

"Oh! Is that the church that does all the prophecy seminars? I've wanted to go to those and haven't been able to yet. When is the next one because I don't want to miss it?"

My member emailed me and said, "When is the next speaker coming because I have this guy's phone number and address and permission to invite him!"

Take your time, be patient and work the system. You will be living in a culture Evangelism Intelligence.

What If Your Church is Negative?

Perhaps you are saying, "That's all fine and good, but my church won't even let me talk about evangelism." Maybe they had a bad experience with an evangelist. Possibly they think evangelism is dead and dying. Or the board is just saying "no" to the idea.

If I had a church – whether I was the pastor, or a member who wanted to do evangelism – that did not believe in evangelism, I would do three main things:

1. I would begin to pray. I would pray for a change of heart. I would pray for people with the gift of evangelism to join me in prayer. I would pray for my church to catch the vision of the Great Commission. I would pray to the Lord of the Harvest to send out workers. Prayer will accomplish much more than any argument at the board meeting.

2. I would next start a cycle of Friendship, Kindness Projects, and Bridge Events and repeat that cycle until my church was willing to come along for the ride of evangelism. If that took three cycles, four, or more, when we finally did follow the plan to a reaping seminar, the harvest will be truly great.

3. I would begin to train members to give Bible studies, visit, and how to share their faith. This accomplishes two things: 1) It creates a group of people who are looking forward to the next reaping/evangelistic event, and 2) if the church continues to say "no" your church has a team that is actively reaching the community anyway.

When my family moved to Colorado to church plant, our conference gave us three years to become "viable" or become part of a district. In other words, if we did not make it work, quickly, we would be part of a two or three church district where my time would be divided. The magic numbers we were striving to hit were about 200 in attendance and about $250,000 in tithe.

Our church grew almost immediately to 100 people. However, we stalled for nearly two years as we refined what we did and how we did it. I remember trying to figure it out and coming up short. One day I concluded the reasons why and that evening went to my leadership team with a request.

I reminded them again what the deadline looming against us in a matter of one year. I told them, "We have $70,000 in the bank. Let's *bet the farm on reaching lost people*. Let's stop spending money on ourselves. Let's stop spending it on equipment. Let's bet everything we have on reaching lost people. Hold nothing back. In the end, if it does not work, we'll know we did everything we could."

They said yes! The next week I went to my four key leaders and told them I wanted to bring an evangelist by the name of Dan Bentzinger. Their response was, "We don't really like the five-nights-per-week thing." "Isn't there some other way?" "We'd really rather not."

I walked away and told my wife, they are against it. We were a little discouraged, but we committed it to prayer and when I met with my core four leaders the next week I realized that for the last two plus years, we had been building a culture of evangelism and I walked into that meeting and said, "We really need to do this." They agreed this time and we did it.

The week before we started, Dan Bentzinger told me we would have about 350 people opening night because of the amount of advertising we had sent. Yet we had rented the Civic Auditorium in Greeley, CO. It was the only auditorium we could get. It sat 850 people on the lower level. We were worried about the empty space scaring people away. But we moved forward in faith.

Opening night, a miracle happened. We had over 750 people there. We ended up baptizing 50 people. Twenty-five of those people came to my church and twenty-five to our sister church who was also helping. So, we added those twenty-five people, and our attendance went up by 75+. We spent every dime we had on it, the whole $70,000. We really did *bet the farm*, but in the end, we had $90,000 in the bank! We never have figured out how God did the math in our attendance and bank statement. But we rejoiced anyway!

Before the seminar started, three friends cornered me in the kitchen at our small group meeting. They were there to tell me that the traditional seminars were not going to work. They wanted me to pull the plug and stop it. These were my best friends and they did not see it working. The meeting with them got kind of heated because I would not back down, I would not pull the plug.

All three of those friends pulled away from me in the month leading up to the seminar. I was hurt, but I was also determined. After it was over, the success was not only unexplainable, but also not hidden to anyone. My one friend, Shane, called Gail and I to his home and he and his wife, Amy, apologized and said, "We were wrong. It did work." Shane later became a pastor and is now successfully pastoring in the Upper Columbia Conference.

8

The Role of the Church Members

George, my head elder, came out of the seminar. We were packed out. This was the seminar I mentioned earlier where our church sat 250 people and we had over 350 opening night. George's eyes were huge. He said, "This is incredible, I've never heard some of this stuff before!"

My response was classic for me, because my heart is more about reaching lost people than anything else. I said, "But you've heard most of this before. So, pray for those people who have never heard it before! This is new and scary, life-changing information for them!"

George looked at me, cocked his head, and said, "Oh yeah." Then he went back in the church auditorium for the remainder of the meeting. It was clear, he had never thought of that before. Yet, to his credit, he became an active pray-er through those meetings and subsequent meetings we held that kept us headed in the right direction.

I am always struck by the fact that the Adventists like to come to the meetings for the same reasons the guests come. They want to hear something new. They want to see what the newest take on Bible prophecy is happening. However, I am pretty sure that 90% of the information they hear will be relatively identical to the previous ten seminars they heard.

In 1 Corinthians 14, Paul makes an argument that prophecy is for the nonbeliever to help them understand that God and scripture is true. Yet, as Adventists, we have a tendency to think that prophecy is the deep things. I tell my church, prophecy is for the beginner and if you are following the prophecy speakers around hoping to learn more, you need to begin focusing on the meatier things of the Christian faith – like walking the walk, having personal devotions, growing to be like Christ.

It is my contention that the role of the members is different than the role of the guests. I see the role of members in three different partner categories. These partners are: Serving, Supporting, and Praying.

Serving

We can do evangelism with about 10-15 people, but that is a minimalist approach. It's been proven repeatedly, the more Adventists we have at the seminar, the more baptisms we will have in the end. There are plenty of places to serve to help fill this category:

- Greeter Team
- Usher Team
- Row Hosts
- Clean Up Team
- Refreshments Team
- Mailing Team
- Open and Closing Team(s)
- Materials Team
- Advertising Team
- Planning Team

We can take a minimalist approach, but we run the risk of 1) burning people out and 2) being selfish with the opportunity to serve. When we get more people involved, it allows us to use the established people to train new people to take on the task someday. Additionally, when people serve without a team, there are blind spots that get left undone. There are plenty of service opportunities in an evangelistic event that help everyone carry a light load.

Supporting

Support comes in a variety of ways. Here are the ways we find people support the evangelistic efforts at our church:

- *They are inviters* – inviting people to come to church, to come to the meetings, to come to various events. People who are inviters are the best advertising any church can have. We are looking for 1-3/1000 response from our brochures, but when a member invites someone, the response rate is 1/10.
    - *This is so big and cannot be emphasized enough. We need a team of inviters!*
- *They are givers* – people who give to support evangelism in their regular, monthly giving are supporting evangelism by allowing us to do it at the proper level rather than on a 1950s budget as mentioned earlier. IT takes funds and givers are a HUGE part of what evangelism gets done.
    - *On a bit of aside note, as you do evangelism, and it becomes effective, you can expect the givers to begin giving more.*
- *They are people meeters* – Some of these people come to the seminar with the specific purpose of sitting in the meetings and getting to know the people around them. They learn names, they ask questions, the become friends so the new people can settle in once they get baptized.
- *They are teachers* – They can also help by giving Bible Studies before the seminar, or after the seminar with people.

These support people are valuable to the seminar's success. It allows us to have people there, to have the funds to do the seminar properly and to have support and mentoring for the follow-up of any individuals. These people are true supporters of the seminars. Yet, more than supporters, they are the only way the seminar can go forward. Without these people, an evangelistic event will fall flat.

Praying

There are many ways and many places to pray for evangelism. We try to put a team together to pray before the seminar, during the seminar, and following the seminar. We pray for the speaker, for open hearts and listening ears. We pray the people will come, that the speaker will stay healthy.

Certainly, for members who come night-by-night, one of their chief ministry positions is to pray for people as they are confronted with the gospel for the first time, the Sabbath, the antichrist, or other topics we cover. We need a prayer covering to make sure that the Holy Spirit has room to work on hearts.

In the last seminar we did, I was in the back of our auditorium watching as the evangelist was having a call. I watched a lady who was a row host in our meetings. She was obviously agonizing in prayer for someone who would later make a decision. I looked around and saw others in the church who were deep in prayer and I had to smile. I knew these people would eventually give in to God, the devil didn't have control anymore!

What Adventist Members Should Not Do

We could spend a lot of time talking about what members should do. But there are a few important things that a member should not do.

First, if you are attending meetings as an Adventist member. Your jobs are listed above. Your job is to not try to entertain the speaker, nor ask him a bunch of questions. The evangelist's job is very clear – to get new people to join with Christ and his church.

If you absolutely must ask a question, do the evangelist a favor and when you walk to him/her, introduce yourself by saying something like, "Hi, my name is Bob. I'm a member here...." This is a signal that helps the evangelist know who a member is and who is not.

I have seen members who want to take on the speaker about some fine-tuned issue that does not matter. Sometimes members get off on the details, because they think the seminar is about information, rather than decisions.

Recently, a member of another local Adventist church challenged me about who the king of the north was and who the king of the south was. I happened to see it differently than him and he started going off about Ellen White saying we would leave the foundations of Adventism. Inside it was like, "Really? The King of the North is a foundation pillar of Adventism? Really?"

My point is that it took up unnecessary time for me. I needed to find a couple of people that evening before they left, and I did not get to them in a crucial decision time, because someone wanted to argue theology with me. It was not worth it. It was not the time. We can have those conversations another time, but not during the seminar.

Second, do not sit with all your church friends and clump together. Move yourself beyond your comfort zone and go sit by someone you do not even know yet. Really, it's not as painful as it sounds. You would also be amazed at how much a friendly face and smile does to help the evangelist with his/her job.

Third, be the last one to take any handouts. Do not worry about not getting some, the church can either get you something similar, or if you would rather, can order more. Remember, that you are not the target of this seminar, the guests are the target and should be the first to get any handouts. If the church has let it be known that there are no shortages, then by all means, take what you want.

Fourth, when you are asked a question by a non-member, DO NOT get ahead of the speaker. So many members want to introduce a promising prospect to Ellen White, to the Sabbath, the Mark of the Beast, etc. There is a reason the messages are in order. Wait, let the speaker cover the material first. Then check with the speaker or the pastor before giving them even more to read on a subject.

In a recent seminar, our speaker asked for a handout in the middle of his presentation. We did not have very many and the ushers were instructed: "1 per family to the guests first." But they did not do that and I had to go up to several members and ask, "Would you be willing to share your handout with a guest? I will be glad to copy it for you later." Everyone was gracious and readily shared, except one lady who refused, but her husband was quicker than her and snatched it out of her hand and handed it to me. I thanked them profusely as I went to redistribute it. When I talked with her afterwards, she apologized, because she misunderstood my whispering and was more than willing to share.

Here is the conclusion of the role of the members. It is not the pastors who do the ministering, but the members. In my church, if you look on the bulletin for who to contact with phone numbers, it says, "Ministers: Every Member." Evangelism is where this is truly lived out. We need to work together – all of us – to see the kingdom work finished.

9

Conclusion/Epilogue

*"When in our work for God
right methods are energetically
followed, a harvest of souls will
be gathered."[65]*

December 7, 2004 was one of the most memorable days in my life. We gathered the family – 4 kids, mom, dad, grandpa – in the truck and headed off to the mountains to find, cut and bring home a Christmas tree. It was a beautiful snowy day. This was a high day.

After about an hour and a half drive up into the Northern Colorado Rocky Mountains, where were at 9,500 feet above sea level, then about a half hour of searching and hiking, we found our tree. My son and I took turns cutting with the hand saw and my wife took pictures for the memory book. When we finally loaded the new Christmas tree into our truck, we were tired and plenty ready to go home.

Did I mention that my wife was eight and a half months pregnant? Due date was 10-12 days ahead of us. On the way home, contractions began and we began timing them. They were 10-15 minutes apart and getting harder by the minute – literally.

---

[65] White, E. G. (1930). *Messages to Young People* (p. 190). Southern Publishing Association.

We passed two large hospitals on our drive home that could have accommodated us, but not our doctor. So, we headed home, got the kids and the tree and the grandpa all unloaded and went in the house to get ready for the hospital visit to Greeley, CO.

Things changed quickly when Gail emerged from the bathroom saying, "My water just broke!"

To understand this statement, you need to understand history. Some ladies, go out to eat for the evening after their water breaks. Some laugh about it. Historically, when Gail's water breaks, a baby is coming in precisely ten minutes. (We now have 8 kids and this timing issue is precise, every time).

So, Gail asks me, "Do we still go to the hospital or have the baby here at home?" The hospital is 30 minutes away. My answer: "It's easier to sell the van than the house, let's get going! NOW!"

After gathering cameras and other necessary items, we headed out the door. We got exactly three miles down the road when Gail says, "The baby is coming!"

I did a double check and sure enough, that little girl was not waiting anymore to come out. I found the most romantic driveway to have a baby and pulled in. I honked the horn, no one came. I reached for my phone to call 911 and began having a back-and-forth argument about calling 911 first or catching the baby first. I opted for the baby. Good call.

No sooner did I get my hands down there, then the baby came flying down the chute and into my hands. Amazing!

After getting the baby settled in with Gail, I called 911 and said we were on the way. Then I called our doctor, whom I had alerted before we left the house, that he missed out on delivering this one. He is a friend of ours. He was nice, when we arrived at the hospital, the crew of nurses, interns and the doctor met us in the parking lot. They cut the cord, whisked mom and baby away and our doctor said, "Go with them, I'll park your car." I think he still wanted to get paid....

Why do I tell you this very personal story? I am glad you asked.

What would it have been like if I would have told my wife, "No! You keep that baby inside"? What would it have been like if I would have pushed her little head back up the chute and said, "No we are not ready for this. We are not ready and until we get ready we cannot have you here!"

All of that would be extremely silly and extremely harmful to the mother and baby. Yet, this is what happens all the time in churches that refuse to do evangelism. One of the biggest arguments I hear from church members and pastors is that we are not ready for this. I have several questions for these people. 1) When will you be ready? 2) When you get ready, how will you know?

You know what? If you waited until you were completely ready to have kids, you would never have kids. It's the same in the church. If you wait until you are ready for new people, you will never be ready.

Before I was a parent, I did not know how to hold kids. People would ask me if I wanted to hold their baby. I was afraid of dropping the baby. I held it at arms-length. After my first child was born, I knew what needed to happen and held him close and protected him and would have given my life for him at that moment.

It's the same in church. People are never ready for new people until they show up. Then they instinctively know how to help and care for them. The more you have, the more you want them to keep coming also. Another thing I have noticed is that you take a dysfunctional church that is fighting all the time, start doing regular evangelism with them and they stop fighting. They no longer have time to fight. They are busy winning new people, caring for new people, getting new people involved and enjoying church and God again!

You will never get ready in advance. You must jump in and start doing it. Sure, you will make mistakes. Church members will speak out of turn ahead of the evangelist. You will lose a few people on the fringe, you will lose a few new people. But every time you take the step, you are learning and growing.

I will be so bold as to say that churches that are not actively reaching new people and baptizing them, is an unhealthy church. Sure, there are all kinds of evangelistic methods, but if you are not actually winning someone to the Lord on a regular basis, I do not care how big your church is, how much everyone likes it, it is unhealthy and is harmful to the spiritual growth of its members.

Why? We need to be exercising all kinds of spiritual gifts. There are discipleship gifts and evangelism gifts. If we are not using the evangelism gifts, we are creating unhealthy, one dimensional disciples. Much of what some churches call their evangelistic strategy is not. If you are not getting decisions for Christ and seeing baptisms, then it is not evangelism. Part of the definition of evangelize is to convert people. Therefore, if people are not being converted, it is not the fullest picture of what could be.

Is it worth it? Jesus said, go. Evangelism related spiritual gifts are the only gifts that go completely away when Jesus comes again. We will no longer need them. We must utilize them now.

SO WHAT?

A friend of mine and I recently had an online discussion about evangelism. He has read most of the preliminary copies of this book. The discussion basically centered around what evangelism means without the message Adventists have been given. Let me reframe it for you for a moment. If it's not for the message, what makes us different from anyone else?

Obviously, every church should be involved in social issues like feeding the homeless, housing crisis issues, helping the poor, racial injustice, etc. If we aren't doing these things, we are breaking the second great commandment. We need to love people in practical ways, help the hurting, give hope to the flailing and show God's love all around our cities with no strings attached. Most churches do this.

Also, every church should be involved with spiritual issues like teaching people to have a relationship with Jesus, how to grow as a Christian, putting down spiritual roots, how to share their faith, overcoming sin, etc. Nearly all churches do this.

Churches should also be involved in the social and emotional needs of their congregations. This would include things like church socials, building friendships, small groups, and being part of a bigger picture in society and family.

We also need churches who are trying new and creative ways of reaching the lost. We need experiments, we need the gospel preached in many ways and to many groups of people. We must do this too.

Yet, what makes Adventism different? What makes us stand out from those other churches if it is not the message we proclaim?

I have another friend who pastors a contemporary church. He refused to do any kind of public evangelism. His method of evangelism has been kindness projects and his worship service. I ask him occasionally, "What makes you an Adventist congregation?" He stood there with an open mouth. It's got to be more than that we go to church on Saturdays. I could also ask him about the number of converts he's not getting, but I did not. What makes us Adventist is the message.

In an old article from Ministry Magazine, a United Methodist minister by the name of Dean M. Kelley, wrote an article showing the downfall of most mainline denominations. The article was entitled, "How Adventism Can Stop Growing."[66] In this article, Kelley, a Methodist, says when Adventists become like the Methodists, we will stop growing, so he tells us to stick to our conservative message – the kind we proclaim it in our evangelistic meetings. He predicts that when we stop, we will stop growing. Was he a prophet? Could it be that Kelley was right that we are in danger of dying if we stop preaching the message we were called up to preach? I agree with George Knight, when we remove the message, we neuter Adventism.

You see, the church does not save anyone. It's the message we proclaim about Jesus Christ that brings people to the point of salvation. The message confronts them straight on with a decision to follow it or not. Without the message, we are trying to ride the cart into town without a horse hitched up. What's the point of the church without a clear message of the gospel as we understand it?

Therefore, our job is to plant seeds with the message and we can let God water that seed. This message is one built upon the message of Jesus Christ and is about grace that saves and grace that changes us. *"For the grace of God that brings salvation has appeared to all men. It teaches us to say 'No' to ungodliness and worldly passions, and to live self-controlled, upright and godly lives in this present age, while we wait for the blessed hope—the*

---

[66] https://www.ministrymagazine.org/archive/1983/02/how-adventism-can-stop-growing

glorious appearing of our great God and Savior, Jesus Christ"[67]
We really can never know the outcome of what happens when we
plant those seeds.

My friend, Richard Halversen, tells this story. Bob and
Elaine came out to a seminar he was conducting in Baltimore,
MD. They were active in the country music industry, skeptical and
had many questions. Bob and Elaine came to Richard's seminar
early each night and interested enough to sit on the front row.
Richard let the message confront them with truth. They were
baptized at the end of the seminar.

Just like Jesus' parable of the sower in Matthew 13 when
the seed falls on rocky soil, describing when troubles come, people
often fall away. This is what happened to Bob and Elaine. The
troubles of life and indifference set in, and they slowly slipped
away.

It's always hard to watch people slip away. Yet they do.
As a pastor, I understand that I can only do so much. God must be
in charge and lead people. But it's hard to watch them slip away.

Eighteen years later, Richard and his wife, Mary, were in
West Virginia doing a seminar. At the end of one of the first few
nights, a couple came forward and asked, "Do you remember us?"
as they handed him a picture of their baptism 18 years before! Yes,
Richard remembered Bob and Elaine and as he embraced them in a
giant bear hug, Bob informed Richard that he was now an
Adventist pastor in West Virginia and his wife Elaine, was a Bible
Worker.

What a reunion that must have been! There was a huge
gap in the story that Bob and Elaine could fill in as they sat and
talked together.

It's not always a heartwarming story that comes out of
evangelism. For every story I have shared that ended well, I have a
story of people who stopped coming. I could share horror stories
of what evangelists have said up front that made my hair turn gray.
I could share stories of people who have come right along, and in
the end, they decided to not go God's way. It was heartbreaking to
say the least.

---

[67] *The Holy Bible: New International Version.* (1984). (Tt 2:11–13).
Grand Rapids, MI: Zondervan.

What I am reminded of with Bob and Elaine's story above is that you never know. You just never know what is really going on in people's minds. You never know if they will come back or not. I have met many people who now come to my church and have been baptized, who have said, "This is the third or fourth seminar I have been to." They finally decided to become Adventists and follow the message we teach. I know others who mimicked Bob and Elaine's story above.

I have one couple who came to a series I was preaching and they began to come to church. She told me one day, "Over the years, I've been to two of these Adventist seminars."

I investigated further, "What makes you come to church now, as opposed to then?" What she said, blew me away.

"It's what you said about the Sabbath and some of those quotes that you put on the screen. I had never seen them before."

I did not go into the details with her any further, but I knew she had seen them before. We have been preaching the Sabbath and the change of the Sabbath for a long time. The quotes were not new, nor were they original with me. However, what I really heard was, she was now ready for the Holy Spirit to break through. She was ready for the information. She was not before. If we stop preaching that message, we stop reaching people who are ready for the message to be preached to them.

If we would have only done kindness projects, or friendship evangelism, it would not have been enough to break her free from her religious background. But the proclamation message brought her around where she was simply confronted with the truth and she could not turn away.

For me there is a sense of urgency where we should be calling on God for the people in our communities. Psalm 2:8 says "Ask of me, and I will make the nations your inheritance, the ends of the earth your possession."[68] God invites us to pray for people to be won to His kingdom.

Carolyn and Rick recently shared their testimony at my church. They were both raised in the Adventist Church. They met at an Adventist college. They married and were active in church and even went on a three-year mission to the Navajo Indians. Rick

---

[68] *The Holy Bible: New International Version.* (1984). (Ps 2:8). Grand Rapids, MI: Zondervan.

is a pharmacist, Carolyn a nurse practitioner. Somehow, after their mission work, they began to drift. They began to take a vacation from church. Their involvement level slipped. Then they stopped coming to church at all and it lasted for 18 years!

As they slipped away from church, their morals and values began to slip as well. One day, after some stock market ups and downs, Rick thought his portfolio had balanced out appropriately and he was on his way to early retirement. As he walked along one day, he heard that still small voice of God saying directly to him, the words of Proverbs 16:25 "There is a way that seems right to a man, but in the end it leads to death."[69] When Rick heard those words, he got angry. He said to himself, "I don't need any of that!"

Yet, he could not shake the feeling and in the end, he made a decision to start reading his Bible again. They eventually found themselves at our church. They watched the building go up and made fun of it just a few months before. However, an evangelistic meeting was starting the very day they walked into church for the first time in 18 years. They came, they were baptized in a portable baptistery, the first in the church, because the auditorium and baptistery were not finished yet.

They have both been active in our church and have served as elders. Now, Rick is an elder and Carolyn is on our paid staff as a Bible worker. They are invaluable to what happens in this church. They continue to bring people to church with them, invite them to follow Christ, and continue to study and visit with many more.

Evangelism Intelligence has been about showing a better way and a deeper understanding of how and why do evangelism. Yet, no one can guarantee the results. What I continue to find and be encouraged by, is that people are hearing the message and in God's timing they come around. We cannot give up.

I believe we need to empower people to do the work of Christ. *"There are many Christian youth that can do a good work if they will learn lessons in the school of Christ from the great Teacher. Even though pastors, evangelists, and teachers should neglect the seeking of the lost, let not the children and youth*

---

[69] *The Holy Bible: New International Version.* (1984). (Pr 16:25). Grand Rapids, MI: Zondervan.

neglect to be doers of the word. ... "[70] No matter what, we cannot stop.

Why can't we stop? Maybe the reason can be found in the 2016 Word of the Year. The word of year is "'*post-truth'* – an adjective defined as 'relating to or denoting circumstances in which objective facts are less influential in shaping public opinion than appeals to emotion or personal belief.'"[71] Our society lives and breathes cultural relativism. That is simply a way to say that truth is defined by whomever is speaking. You believe what you want, and I will believe what I want. What is true for me, may not be true for you and vice-versa. To a Christian who believes in absolute truth this is hard to cipher.

Listen to this interchange from a 2010 documentary called, "The Nature of Existence."

> ***The Nature of Existence*** is a 2010 documentary that asks and attempts to answer some of life's biggest questions. One of the segments is on truth. One particular scene begins with the word truth on the screen and a drawing of a man with his fingers crossed behind his back as if he is concealing something. The narrator asks questions, and various people answer.
>
> Narrator: Can you define the word *truth?*
>
> Unnamed man: No, I think it's like pornography. You know it when you see it.
>
> Hindu cleric, speaking in his native tongue (subtitles): By worshiping God you can find the truth.
>
> Tao cleric (subtitles): Anything that runs counter to Tao will not be truth.
>
> Narrator: What is truth?
>
> Bobby Gaylor, musician: What people don't want to hear.
>
> Alan F. Segal, professor of religion, Columbia University: When somebody claims to

---

[70] White, E. G. (1930). *Messages to Young People* (p. 180). Southern Publishing Association.
[71] https://en.oxforddictionaries.com/word-of-the-year/word-of-the-year-2016

know the truth, and claims to be able to tell it to you, the first thing you should do is check to see if you still have your watch, because that's the prelude to getting taken.

Jim Murphy, champion drag racer: I've had a pretty messed up childhood, and God gave me the faith of a small child. I totally believe. It's all in my heart. I know my knower knows there's a God, and he's in charge of everything. I just know that. To me that's faith.

Julia Sweeney, author, *Letting Go of God*: In science, you don't use words like *truth*. You say, "Closer to truth."

Irvin Kershner, director, *Star Wars: The Empire Strikes Back*: Only art comes close to trying to answer truth.

Unnamed man: The opposite of faith is a tendency to ask questions.

12-year-old child: I think truth is what we're all searching for, isn't it? Even though, sometimes, it's more fun to search for it than actually find it.[72]

We live currently in a society that is fast moving towards such a relative position of what truth is or is not – depending on who is defining it – but in the end, society is saying truth really does not matter. What matters is how I feel about it. To me, this gives me a sense of urgency. We should be preaching the message while we still can. We should be preaching it while people will still listen. If we truly believe that Jesus is coming soon, then we should be about the work of the kingdom. This is a no-holds barred battle we are in.

And the word of the year is *post-truth*.

---

[72] The Nature of Existence, *DVD, directed by Roger Nygard, 2010, chapter 23: "Truth," 33:44 - 36:11* (retrieved from: http://www.preachingtoday.com/illustrations/2012/march/3031912.html? share=LHrJGJEepya5%2bY7U%2fWupUS5PioC%2bwJLq)

However, Jesus said the truth will set you free![73] He also said there is no way to God except through Him and He defined Himself as the "I am the way, and the truth, and the life."[74] Jesus thought truth mattered. It seems as if we should too.

That truth includes but is not limited to:

- Jesus Christ died for our sins.
- Jesus Christ lived as our example.
- The Sabbath is about God's grace. It reminds us of creation and of His redemption of us.
- The Second Coming is a call to hope for all the evil in this world. It is a hope that evil is conquered by good.
- Death and Hell is a message of grace, about a God that does not torture people for eternity.
- Truth is about Jesus and leads us to renounce our sin and submit our lives to Him.

Evangelism Intelligence begins and ends with that message. I am not sure the doctrines even matter without the message of Jesus Christ front and center. He is the truth we need. We have been called to preach truth, sound teaching, and to do the work of an evangelist – reaching lost people for the kingdom.

I heard a story a long time ago. It was set back in the horse and buggy days. A farmer was away from home on his horse and got caught in a snow storm. He pulled his jacket up and his hat down to protect against the biting cold of the snow and wind.

However, it started blowing harder and more snow. It was worse than being a reindeer in a snow globe. He could not see. As the trail was covered, he had to slow down so he could try to see the indenting in the snow where the trail was. It got to near white-out conditions. The farmer finally crawled down from the horse, so he could walk and lead the horse. He could still kick in the snow and feel the difference between the trail and the grassy areas.

Yet, his feet began to grow cold and numb. Pretty soon he was stumbling because his feet felt like they were stuck in cement.

---

[73] The Holy Bible: English Standard Version. (2016). (Jn 8:31–32). Wheaton: Standard Bible Society.
[74] *The Holy Bible: English Standard Version.* (2016). (Jn 14:6). Wheaton: Standard Bible Society.

It felt like he'd been out there for hours and there was no end in sight. His hands were cold, he was walking in a daze.

The farmer did not know how long he'd been walking when he realized he was no longer hanging onto the reigns and leading the horse. His hands were frostbitten and he did not know when the reigns slipped out of his hands. For the first time, he really got scared because the horse was nowhere to be seen. What would he do without his horse for companionship, for warmth and protection from the cold. With that horse gone, he lost his saddle, his rifle, his blanket everything he needed. The farmer could not even tell which direction he was walking, and he had long ago lost his way.

There was nothing else to do, but to continue on down the way he'd determined was the way. But he was so cold. He stumbled several times and fell into the snow. He was wet, frozen, and tired. He was so tired. And he was cold. So cold. The farmer could not feel his feet anymore. He could not feel his hands. His legs were numb and felt like tree stumps as he tried to walk.

It was useless to go on. He finally decided he would hole-up under a tree and take a short nap. He had to warm up and sleep sounded like it would make him warmer. He made a little dug out from the wind and lay down shivering. He was just about to fall asleep when he heard something. What was that?

"Help!" There it was again! It was someone calling for help. Someone else was out there in the snow with him. The farmer got up and started calling back. He hurried along, never once thinking about his feet or hands. He was no longer tired. He found the man who was calling for help."

"What happened?"

"I came out to my field to gather a stray cow in and I got lost in the storm. I then slipped and fell and broke my leg, I think. If you hadn't come along, I would have died. I couldn't get up to get to my house. It's about 50 yards that direction."

The farmer was saved, by someone else who needed help.

In saving others, we save ourselves. "No sooner does one come to Christ than there is born in his heart a desire to make known to others what a precious friend he has found in Jesus...."[75]

---

[75] White, E. G. (1892). *Steps to Christ* (p. 78). Pacific Press Publishing Association.

We have a work to do – evangelism – and if we will do it, we will find we too are saved in the process.

CONTACT

If you'd like to talk more about coaching, or the details of this book, please feel free to contact me via email at:

coachenator@gmail.com

or you can look at my blog at:

http://rogerwalter.wordpress.com

Appendix
Helpful Documents

Evangelism Schedule:

Pre-Work

    a.   Friendship Evangelism *(taught regularly and shared regularly) – Constant by members and leaders*

    b.   Kindness Evangelism – Random Acts of Kindness - *Monthly*

    c.   Service Projects – Community Clean-up, Neighbor Helping, etc. – *Quarterly*

    d.   Bible Study Mailing Cards – *2-3 Months before*

    e.   VBS/FLAG Camp – *2 Months before*

    f.   Bridge Events – Cooking Schools, Health Clinics, Money Management Classes, Concerts, etc. – *1-3 months before.*

    g.   Follow Reaping Meeting System that begins 6 months before any seminar – *to determine budget, location, materials, teams, training, etc.*

Evangelistic Event

    h.   Mail to as large of budget as possible

    i.   Advertise on at least three legs – Newspaper, Radio, TV and Mail (others too?)

    j.   Visitation, literature,

Follow-up

    k.   Bible Marking Class – Pastor Taught – 12-14 weeks repeated what was taught in the seminar – slower pace, Q&A, More literature, focused prayer time, teach about some of the systems and lifestyle issues of Adventism (tithe, vegetarianism, structure, etc.) – *Immediately following*

    l.   Small Groups/Community Groups – out of the baptismal candidates and the almost people, we form new groups with trained leaders. They are not integrated into old groups, but new groups started. – *Immediately following*

m. Targeted preaching to new people – *Lasts for 6-8 weeks*

n. Targeted visitation program to the New People – *lasts for 6-12 months*

o. New Members Orientation Class – where people are introduced to Community Groups, Spiritual Gifts, Tithing/Offering, Involvement, Mission/Vision of the Church, LIFE Journals, etc. – *Offer twice within 6 weeks after seminar*

p. Commitment to be involved in the process

Reaping Meetings – List of Jobs

- Children's Ministry Coordinator – 1
  - Nightly Leaders – 1
  - Nightly Helpers – 2, 3
  - Music Person(s) – 1+
- Book and Tape Table – 2, 3
- Greeters – 4, 5 opening night, 3 every night after that (depending on size of auditorium)
- Auditorium Set Up – 2-3
- Cleaning/Close-up – 2-3/night
- Visitation Team – 5-7
- Row Hosts – 1 per 25 chairs
- Refreshments – 2 per night/week
- Announcements – 3
- Ushers for Offering – 2-4 per section (depending on size of section)
- Registration Table – 3-4 People

Evangelism Seminar System 3.0

■ Pastoral Staff, ◯ Office Staff, ◆ Evangelism Team

1. **6 Months Before** ◆
   a. Evangelism Team Develops Preliminary Budget
   b. Determine speaker *(if not before)*
2. **4 Months Before** ◆
   a. Make Advertising Strategy
      i. Going to just do mailing?
      ii. Doing TV, Radio, or Newspaper too?
      iii. Billboards?
      iv. Websites, Social Media?
   b. Determine Zip Codes for Mailing
   c. Determine Brochure Used
      i. Finalize dates
      ii. Finalize titles of ALL meetings, especially opening nights
   d. Conduct a Bridge Event ◆
3. **2 Months Before** ◆◯
   a. Team Development
      i. Teams Needed:
         1. Children's Ministry Coordinator (1) Children's Team (2-4/week)
         2. Book and Tape Table (1-2)
         3. Greeters (4-5 opening 2-3 nights, 3 after that)
         4. Set Up Team (3-7 people)
         5. Cleaning Team (2-5 people)
         6. Visitation Teams (3-5 teams of 2)
         7. Refreshments (2 per week)
         8. Announcements (3)
         9. Ushers (2 per section)
         10. Registration Table (4-6 opening 2-3 nights, 2-4 after that)
         11. (Optional) Row Hosts (1/2 rows of pews)
   b. Order Brochures ◯
   c. Order Materials, handouts, Bibles, etc. ◯
   d. Conduct a Bridge Event ◆
4. **1 Month Before** ◆◯
   a. Teams Trained for their respective positions – hand out their Delegation Sheets, and go over it with the leader
   b. Mailing to last 3-4 series prepared *(will be mailed out two weeks in advance of seminar)*
   c. Determine nightly food schedule
5. **3 Weeks Before** ◆
   a. Visit the previous Baptized people and invite them back or invite them to invite new people to come.

6. **2 Weeks Before**
   a. Mail to prior series attendees ◎
   b. offerings, and what handouts happen at each night. ◎
   c. Prepare database – titles, night numbers, etc. Test! Test! Test! ◎
   d. Schedule finished for follow-up to seminar – visitation schedule, Community Group leaders found
   e.
7. **1 Week Before**
   a. Make Sure all Schedules are finalized and help fill in any as needed ◎
8. **1-2 Days Before** ◈◎
   a. Dress Rehearsal
9. **Nightly** ◈◎
   a. Small Group Testimonials generic, leading up to testimonies of the Sabbath
   b. New Small Group Leaders meet with Interests and get to know them to invite to group
   c. Offerings as called for
   d. Ushers as needed for cards, calls, offerings, etc. – should be planned out 2-3 weeks before seminar begins
   e. Social time at least once/week
   f. Nightly printout IMMEDIATELY AFTER the evening's meeting, of that night's attendance.
10. **Last Week of Seminar** ◈
    a. Small Group Leaders begin inviting the key guests and going easy on those that have not decided yet.
    b. Begin inviting to Bible Marking Class
    c. Prepare the follow-up Flier
11. **1 Week after** ◎
    a. Begin Bible Marking Class
    b. Follow-up System Begun
12. **1 Month afterwards** ◎◈
    a. Names in Fellowship1 Database as needed
    b. Names in future mailing list
    c. Review Conducted of this seminar ◈

The Church Year

- Training/Discipleship/Bridge Events (Jan-Mar 15)

- Evangelism (Mar 15-April 30)

- Discipleship (May-Jun)

- Training/Bridge/Discipleship/VBS Events (Jun 15-Sept 10)

- Evangelism (Sep 15-Oct 15)

- Discipleship (Nov-Dec)

Evangelism Checklist

1. Order amidst Chaos
    a. WHY: "God is a God of order. Everything connected with heaven is in perfect order; subjection and thorough discipline mark the movements of the angelic host. Success can only attend order and harmonious action. God requires order and system in His work now no less than in the days of Israel. All who are working for Him are to labor intelligently, not in a careless, haphazard manner. He would have his work done with faith and exactness, that He may place the seal of His approval upon it." PP 376
2. Volunteers
    a. Ministry descriptions completed
    b. Delegation worksheets completed
    c. Teams Needed
        i. Data Entry
        ii. Open and Closing
        iii. Announcement Slides
        iv. Row Host
        v. Sales – book, CD, DVDs
        vi. Children's ministry
        vii. Cleaning team
        viii. Visitation team
        ix. Refreshment team
        x. Announcement team
        xi. Ushers
        xii. Registration table
        xiii. Drop-off Visitation Team
        xiv. Phone calling team
        xv. Mailing team
    d. Signed up
    e. Scheduled
    f. Communicated with Regularly
    g. Thanked Appropriately
3. Materials
    a. What is the budget for materials
    b. What materials are needed for each night
    c. What materials are needed for sales table

       d. When is it ordered

       e. Who orders

       f. When is the order and materials list finalized

       g. Who are they handed out – row hosts, greeters, ushers, other

4. Budget

       a. Money requests turned into Oregon Conference by October 15 of each year

       b. Determine how much in our current fund at local church

       c. How much money do we need for this seminar

           i. Children's programming

           ii. Materials and handouts

           iii. Advertising

           iv. Speaker fees

           v. Clothing

           vi. Miscellaneous

           vii. Bibles

           viii. Follow-up (may be able to absorb this out of normal church budget)

           ix. Thank you's

           x. Food/refreshments

           xi. Paying people to help

           xii. How much can be absorbed in the normal church budget – how much needs to be absorbed

       d. How much do we need to raise (funds needed – funds from conference – funds in hand = need)

       e.

5. Speaker

       a. Schedule speaker (most are 2-3 years out, get on it early)

       b. Referencing

       c. Deposit

       d. Contract

       e. Costs against budget

       f. Do we need him/her to come in for a pre-meeting?

6. Advertising

       a. Time frame

       b. Budget

    c. Brochures designed (Marcelo, drop-dead date – 6-8 weeks out)

    d. Brochures ordered (6 weeks in advance)

    e. How many brochures do we need in the congregation (2-3 weeks bulletin inserts, plus extra)

    f. Radio

    g. TV

    h. Newspaper

    i. Which supplier of brochures (SermonView, Color Press, Hamblin, Other)

    j. Mail to former Attendees

        i. Print Labels out of previous meetings immediately after those meetings

        ii. Print last two mailing lists at the same time

        iii. Put labels in a folder to wait

        iv. Write a letter of invitation to new seminar 1 month before new meetings begin

        v. Give to mailing team 3 weeks before seminar begins

        vi. Put in mail 2 weeks before seminar begins

        vii. Repeat at end of seminar.

7. Training Materials

    a. See Clouzet Materials

    b. Music

    c. Setup

    d. Prayer focus

    e. Team building

    f. More people involved, more who come, more changed lives

8. Thank You's

    a. Determine budget

    b. Determine level of involvement

    c. Gift cards

    d. Thank you notes

    e. All involved should be thanked on some level. Some receive greater thanks

9. Pastors Involvement

    a. Speaker Helper

    b. Float and meet people after night 3

    c. Learn people's names – MOST important

    d. Help as assigned or as needed

    e. Be flexible.

10. Food

    a. Have a distinct budget (fixed nightly/person, or overall budget)

    b. Vary the people who do it

    c. Get them extra help for set-up and tear down

    d. Non-greasy foods

    e. Non-staining foods

    f. No popcorn

    g. Give a definite time frame – how much time it will take per night – when asking

    h. Give a definite schedule of what days of the week are needed

    i. Include hours/week in ministry description

    j. This is a job that takes many hands to do it well. Do not leave it to one or two people.

11. Prayer

    a. Gather team nightly at 45 minutes before meeting to pray.

    b. All serving should be part of this gathering – it's important.

        i. This is a debrief time, instructional time too

    c. Pray with the speaker before he goes on stage

    d. There is never enough prayer

    e. Do we need a "40 days of prayer" like campaign before hand?

    f. Is there a prayer team – who it is their specific job to pray during the meetings, with the team, and with the speaker.

12. Follow-Up

13. Communication

    a. Communicate with Row Hosts in a weekly meeting – about what's happening, how they are doing, what to expect, what their role will be this coming week.

    b. Regular emails to the team helping before, during and after

      c. Nightly - With speaker – about needs, people coming, team helping, what is coming, what is/is not happening, etc. – nightly

      d. Encouraging words

      e. With office help

      f. With database help

14. Last Minute Plans

      a. We need a plan for how to deal with last minute things

          i. Who makes the decision

          ii. How late is too late to deal with it

          iii. Who is the go-to person

          iv. Who is the can-do person?

          v. Other....

15. Nightly Meetings

      a. Dress Rehearsal

16. Pre-Work System

      a. Bridge Events

      b. Mail to Former Attendees

      c. Congregational Involvement

17. Systems

18. Timeline Checklist

      a. 6 months before

      b. 4 months before

      c. 2 months before

      d. 1 month before

      e. 3 weeks before

      f. 2 weeks before

      g. 1 week before

      h. 1-2 days before

      i. Last Week of Seminar

      j. 1 Week After

      k. 1 Month After

ABOUT THE AUTHOR

Roger Walter thoroughly enjoys life with Gail, his wife of 30 years and their family. They have eight children and one son-in-law, because they believe in growing the church any way they can! Together they love rock-climbing, hiking, building, photography, and reaching lost people. He is the Lead Pastor at the Adventist Community Church in Vancouver, WA (USA). He is also the Outreach Director for the Oregon Conference which means he primarily focuses on evangelism, church planting and coaching pastors. Roger has an earned doctorate in preaching from Andrews University.

BOOK COVER

Book cover and design by Summer Walter and Gail Walter

Made in the USA
San Bernardino, CA
19 December 2018